Bloody Poetry

'Brenton is, in fact, doing something markedly ambitious in this phantasmagoric play. He is celebrating the idea of the committed artist who seeks to stir and provoke sullen, defeated, bourgeois England. At the same time with clear-eyed honesty, he shows how difficult it is to upset the moral order.'

Michael Billington, *Guardian*

Bloody Poetry received its world première by the Foco Novo Theatre Company at the Haymarket Theatre, Leicester in autumn 1984 before transferring to the Hampstead Theatre, London.

HOWARD BRENTON

Howard Brenton was born in Portsmouth in 1942 and educated in Chichester and at St Catherine's College, Cambridge. In 1968 he joined the Brighton Combination as an actor and writer, and in 1969 he joined David Hare and Tony Bicât in Portable Theatre. His first full-length play was *Revenge* (1969) which was performed at the Royal Court Upstairs; this was followed by *Hitler Dances* (1972); *Magnificence* (1973); *Brassneck* (with David Hare, 1973); *The Churchill Play* (1974); *Weapons of Happiness* (winner of the Evening Standard Award, 1976); *Epsom Downs* (1977); *Sore Throats* (1979); *The Life of Galileo* (from Bertolt Brecht, 1980); *The Romans in Britain* (1980); *Thirteenth Night* (1981); *Danton's Death* (from Büchner, 1982); *The Genius* (1983); *Bloody Poetry* (1984); *Desert of Lies* (1984); *Pravda* (with David Hare, 1985); *Greenland* (1988); *Iranian Nights* (with Tariq Ali, 1989). His four-part thriller *Dead Head* was broadcast by BBC2 in 1986. A novel, *Diving for Pearls* was published in 1989.

D0582542

A METHUEN MODERN PLAY

First published in Great Britain in 1985
by Methuen London Ltd.
Revised and reprinted for the Royal Court Writers series, 1988.
Revised and reprinted for this edition, 1989.
Copyright © 1985, 1988, 1989 by Howard Brenton

British Library Cataloguing in Publication Data

Brenton, Howard
   Bloody Poetry. ——(Methuen modern plays)
   1. Title
   822'.914   PR6052.R426

ISBN 0-413-58350-3

Set in 10pt Journal by Words & Pictures Ltd,
Thornton Heath, Surrey CR4 8JG

Printed and bound in Great Britain by
Cox & Wyman Ltd, Reading

Howard Brenton

Bloody
POETRY

METHUEN DRAMA

The People in the Play

BYRON

Lord George Gordon Byron was born in 1788, of 'Mad Jack' Byron, a
Captain in The Guards, and Catherine Gordon, a Scottish heiress descended
from James I of Scotland. At birth his right foot was deformed, a disability
he fought against all his life with violent exercise. Described by a lover,
Lady Caroline Lamb, as 'Mad, bad and dangerous to know', he was the
most fashionable and commercially successful poet of his day, earning
huge sums for his long poems *Childe Harold* and *Don Juan*. To his
contemporaries he was both idol and bogeyman, a profligate talent with a
rakish reputation — he once said 'What I earn by my brains, I spend by my
bollocks'. Like Oscar Wilde eighty years later, he was the victim of a sexual
scandal, a love affair with his half-sister Augusta Leigh. Because of it he left
England in 1816 and never returned. That year he met Shelley for the first
time at Secheron on Lake Geneva, Switzerland. A rebel by temperament
rather than by intellect, he died in 1824 of a marsh fever at Missolonghi,
while organising a brigade in support of the Greek forces in the ultimately
successful Greek Revolution against Turkish rule.

BYSSHE

Percy Bysshe Shelley was born in 1792 the son of Sir Timothy Shelley, a minor aristocrat and country squire. With, for some, the exception of John Milton, he is the greatest poet in the language after Shakespeare. He was educated at Eton, where he fought remorseless bullying with ferocious fits of temper. In 1811 he was sent down from Oxford University for writing a pamphlet, *The Necessity of Atheism*, with his friend T.J. Hogg. In 1812 he travelled to Dublin where he published his *Address To The Irish People*, a tract against British rule in Ireland. His early poem *Queen Mab*, though it sold less than two hundred copies in his life-time, became an inspirational text for early trade unionists and the Chartist Movement. Among his major poems are *Hymn To Intellectual Beauty* and *Mont Blanc* (1816); *Julian And Maddalo* (1818) which dramatises an argument with Byron about human nature; *Prometheus Unbound* (1818-19) which rivals *Paradise Lost* in ambition and breadth of vision; *The Mask Of Anarchy* (1819), written in protest at the Peterloo Massacre; *Epipyschidion* (1821), a complex personal meditation on love, and the unfinished allegory *The Triumph of Life* (1822). He was drowned in a boating accident in the Gulf of Spezia, Italy, on 8th July, 1822 — he was twenty-nine years old. His body was recovered and burnt on the beach in the presence of a few friends, Byron among them.

MARY

Mary Godwin was the daughter of Mary Woolstonecraft, the author of *The Vindication Of The Rights Of Women* and William Godwin, the author of *Enquiry Concerning Political Justice* — it was a famous family of radical political thinkers. Mary's mother died giving birth to her: her father doted on his daughter obsessively. Mary met Shelley, then married to Harriet, in 1813: she was the first to declare love. With Claire, they eloped to the continent. William Godwin's wrath at this out-break of 'free love' amongst his family, the preaching of which he preferred to the practice, was abated by a series of loans from Shelley which he, in turn, had to borrow money to pay. She was the author of *Frankenstein, or The Modern Prometheus*, a profound parable attacking some basic beliefs of the Romantic Movement, which has been sadly travestied by 20th century horror films. After Shelley's death she gradually became estranged from Claire and Shelley's friends, who accused her bitterly of suppressions and omissions in her publications of Shelley's work. Nevertheless her notes to the poems are a lucid and militant defence of the poetry and their life together. She died in 1851.

CLAIRE

When the play opens Claire Clairemont is eighteen. She was christened Jane, but changed her name to Claire because it means 'light'. Her mother married William Godwin in 1803, his second wife — she and Mary Godwin were therefore sisters by marriage. The passionate, volatile triangular relationship between Claire, Mary and Shelley began at the same time Mary and Shelley became lovers. Claire's mother believed that Shelley had seduced Claire with Mary's connivance. Claire was a free-thinker and a utopian who wanted to create what she called 'The subterranean community of women'. Her surviving letters do not do justice to the tenacity and optimism with which she lived her life. Her affair with Byron began in April, 1816 — their child Allegra was born the following year. A year after Shelley's death she travelled to Russia, taking a post as a governess in Moscow. She never married and died, in genteel poverty, in Florence in 1879. Her refusal in old age to give Shelley's love letters to an intrusive American academic inspired Henry James to write *The Aspern Papers*.

HARRIET

Harriet was the daughter of John Westbrook, a retired merchant and coffee house proprietor. She met Shelley through her friendship with his sisters. In 1811, when sixteen years old, she eloped to Scotland with the nineteen year-old Shelley where they married against her father's wishes. She accompanied Shelley to Dublin and helped him distribute anti-British, pro-Fenian material. The marriage came under strain on the birth of their first child, Ianthe, in 1813. Shelley left her for Mary Godwin when she was four months pregnant with their second child, a boy, Charles, born in 1814. She fought fiercely to save the marriage, travelling to London to confront Mary, then for her young family threatening Shelley with a private prosecution for atheism if he did not increase the allowance for the children. In the summer of 1816 she sent the children to the country to be looked after by a clergyman and cut her ties with her family to live with an army officer. When he was posted to India she found herself penniless and pregnant. She drowned herself in the Serpentine, London, in December 1816.

POLIDORI

Doctor John William Polidori graduated from Edinburgh University at the age of nineteen with a degree in medicine and a fluent grasp of French and Italian. He accompanied Byron on the flight to Europe in 1816 as his secretary and personal physician. At the same time, without asking Byron's permission, he accepted 500 guineas from John Murray, Byron's publisher, to write an account of the journey. A vain, highly strung young man, he became the butt of Shelley, Mary and Byron's at times cruel sense of fun. He wrote plays which they mercilessly ridiculed. He was accident prone — paying court to Mary one day he fell over and broke his ankle. Biographers are in his debt for his sensational account of the night of 18th June, 1816, when talk of ghosts and Byron's reading of Coleridge's *Christabel* induced a violent fit in Shelley. Mary, with some malice, used his name for Frankenstein's evil teacher — perhaps out of revenge Polidori claimed, untruthfully, to have given her the plot in the first place. He shot himself in 1827, because of gambling debts.

Bloody Poetry was commissioned by Foco Novo Theatre Company and was first presented at the Haymarket Theatre, Leicester on 1 October 1984, with the following cast:

PERCY BYSSHE SHELLEY	Valentine Pelka
MARY SHELLEY	Fiona Shaw
CLAIRE CLAIREMONT	Jane Gurnett
GEORGE, THE LORD BYRON	James Aubrey
DR WILLIAM POLIDORI	William Gaminara
HARRIET WESTBROOK, later her GHOST	Sue Burton
VOICE	a member of the company

Director Roland Rees
Assistant to the Director Marina Caldarone
Designer Poppy Mitchell
Costumes Sheelagh Killeen
Composer and Musical Director Andrew Dickson
Lighting by Richard Moffatt
Sound by Paul Bull

This production transferred to the Hampstead Theatre, London, where it was first performed on 31 October 1984.

The play takes place between the summers of 1816 and 1822 in Switzerland, England and Italy.

'Shelley's life seems more a haunting than a history.'
                       Shelley: The Pursuit, Richard Holmes

ACT ONE

Scene One

BYSSHE
Flickering shadows, the window of a coach.

BYSSHE. The Alps. Switzerland. The coach. Aching bones.
Dirty clothes. Hotel rooms we cannot afford. Above us —

Far, far above, piercing the infinite sky
Mont Blanc appears, — still, snowy and serene —
Its subject mountains their unearthly forms
Pile around it, ice and rock; broad vales between
Of frozen floods, unfathomable deeps,
Blue as the overhanging heaven —

Bump, bump, bump — dejected thoughts. In exile.

He laughs.

The flight out of England, Mary! With little William, and
Claire, what an unholy, holy family! We little band of
atheistical perverts, free-lovers, we poeticals — leaving England.

England, England.
A people starved and stabbed in the untilled field.
Rulers who neither see, nor feel, nor know
But leech-like to their fainting country cling,
Til they drop, blind in blood.

Bump, bump, bump —

Men of England, wherefore plough
For the lords who lay ye low?
Wherefore weave with toil and care
The rich robes your tyrants wear?

Bump, bump, bump, bump, bump, bump!

The living frame which sustains my soul
Is sinking beneath the fierce control
Down through the lampless deep of song
I am drawn and driven along

Bump bump, wave on wave —

This world is the mother of all we know,
This world is the mother of all we feel —

Waves.

The shore of Lake Geneva. The 25th of May, eighteen hundred and sixteen.

Scene Two

Beach. Lake Geneva. BYSSHE, MARY *and* CLAIRE. MARY *and* CLAIRE *looking out.* BYSSHE *pacing back and forth at the back.*

CLAIRE. There!

In that boat! His head against the light.

BYSSHE *stops, looks briefly, then continues to pace.*

The head of a god, the head of Lord Byron.

MARY *winces.*

MARY. It is the head of a local fisherman, out for the fish that will be fresh on the menus of expensive restaurants tonight. I do not think the Lord Byron is out catching with his own hands what he may well pay excessively to eat.

A silence.

CLAIRE. It was you and Bysshe who wanted this meeting. It was you who encouraged me to engineer it. It was you who wished to throw yourselves at the feet of England's greatest living poet.

MARY *glances at* BYSSHE *who snorts angrily.*

I knew he would come to this hotel. It was I who sat up late last night, and heard his coach.

MARY. His Lordship's coach. It is — an ostentatious vehicle.

CLAIRE. I have ridden in it. It has a bed!

MARY. For two, of course —

CLAIRE. Shelves lined with books and is, naturally, very well stocked with wines.

MARY. Naturally. A library, bedroom and bar-room on wheels. What more could a poet desire?

CLAIRE. I — sent him a letter. At two o'clock this morning.

MARY. Claire, you did not —

CLAIRE. I sent a letter to my lover, yes.

MARY. Oh Claire my dear, my dear.

CLAIRE. I am not ashamed.

MARY. No.

A silence.

No, you are not.

CLAIRE. I told him Bysshe and we were here.

MARY. He did not rush to meet us at breakfast.

CLAIRE. His footman said he had gone into Geneva, to shop.
For —

She picks at her nails.

For his dogs.

MARY. For dog-food?

CLAIRE. But if we walk on the beach he will come off the lake.
I saw him, putting out in a boat. He will come off the lake,
he will!

MARY. We wait ten days for him in a hotel, at a ruinous price.
The Olympian god of English poetry arrives, ignores us and
goes to buy dog-food —

CLAIRE. He is most anxious that, after a journey, his dogs be
fed fine meat.

MARY sighs and looks out over the lake.

Mary?

Nothing from MARY.

This is not like you, to be so — uneasy.

MARY. I —

CLAIRE. What?

MARY. No matter.

CLAIRE. What?

MARY. I — still have dreams of the journey here.

CLAIRE. The mountains were beautiful.

MARY. They were desolate.

CLAIRE, irritated.

CLAIRE. Oh we must not — ! Be dejected, spiral down, fall into dejection and — hurt each other, we must not.

MARY. No.

A silence.

No.

CLAIRE. We are privileged to make this journey. We are privileged to stand on this beach, and see George Byron and Bysshe Shelley meet. It will be history!

MARY. Well. We will all write it up in our diaries, surely. And read each other's accounts, secretly. What else is there to do?

Looking out over the lake.

Drifting across Europe. Spying on each other's confessions.

CLAIRE. The two poets meet on a beach. Light blazes off the water, behind them. In their exile, they embrace. It will be like a statue. And I have been the lover of one, and am the lover of the other.

A toss of the head.

All of us, we will become magnificent. The men and the women of the future will thank us. We are their great experiment. We will find out how to live and love, without fear.

MARY. If the money does not run out.

CLAIRE. Your sarcasm's horrible Mary, I hate it, I hate it, I have never heard it before.

MARY. I told you — the journey has made me — cold. Inside.

CLAIRE. Horribly unfair! When you heard that George and I —

With a toss of her head.

The Lord Byron and I had made love, your first thought was — 'Oh good. Claire will arrange a meeting between Bysshe and him.' No, 'sister'? Did you not have, at once, that scheme? In your notoriously strong, womanly mind —

MARY. Forgive me Claire. Yes.

CLAIRE. Yes! Then keep in mind, I lifted my skirt, for this.

Bitter, suddenly near to tears.

In a hotel room, ten miles from London, I lifted my skirt. For

the good of English poetry? Long live poetry, yes, Mary? He
has very bad teeth, George Byron, you know. His teeth they
are not good. And he has the scar marks of boils on his body,
from something he caught from little boys in Turkey, he
told me.

MARY. Claire, I do want them to meet, I want us all to meet.
The attraction is too strong, a like-mind. In England they want
to hang us all. Bad reviews are not good enough for our
enemies, they would like a public execution.

She looks at CLAIRE.

You do know that the Home Office has set up secret
committees. That they are investigating Bysshe.

CLAIRE. Oh, he'll love that (*To* BYSSHE.) You'd love to be
last seen, shouting before a firing squad on Tower Hill.
Wouldn't you Bysshe!

BYSSHE *turns away.* CLAIRE, *quoting:*

We tread
On fire! The avenging Power his hell on earth hath spread!

MARY. Quite. They want to hang, draw and quarter what
we stand for. And the loneliness is great, is it not, my
dear. So —

A shrug, a laugh.

Let us play at gods and goddesses, moving in brilliant light on
a beach by a lake, in dresses of white silk flowing about limbs,
we statues. But we must not forget that statues — do not eat,
they do not have bank accounts overdrawn by thousands of
pounds, they do not —

With a glance at BYSSHE.

— have lungs of mucus and blood, they do not —

She looks at CLAIRE, *pauses.*

— have women's wombs.

CLAIRE. I don't care, I don't care, I don't care.

MARY. Nor do I.

They glance at each other, a giggle.

CLAIRE. I am going to live it.

MARY. Yes.

CLAIRE. I am going to be loved, happy and free.

MARY. Yes.

Depression.

Yes.

CLAIRE. Let us draw courage from our appalling reputations. How the world sees us is, like it or not, how we are condemned to live. I think we have no choice in the matter. Good I say, good, good!

She laughs.

Remember what the *Daily Mail* called us?

MARY. All too well.

CLAIRE. 'Shelley's ball girls? Quote — 'Mr Shelley is a bad poet. Like a bad tennis player, his verses forever smash into the net and fall to the ground. But Mr. Shelley is lucky. Two beautiful girls crouch on the sidelines, waiting to pick up his balls'.

MARY. Gutter journalism.

CLAIRE. The real world.

BYRON, *shouting at the back.*

BYRON. Damn you sir — your destiny may be to be eaten by crabs and fishes, but mine is not sir! You are no sailor sir!

The weak voice of POLIDORI *is heard.*

POLIDORI. My Lord I do protest —

BYRON. Blast you, do you — there are people of quality upon the beach, go off sir!

POLIDORI. My Lord!

BYRON. Go off and drown, damn you! I will have none of your damn foolery!

BYRON *storms down up onto the stage. He limps. He turns and shouts.*

Off! T'Neptune! A watery trident up your arsehole sir!

Turns to CLAIRE. *Charm.*

Claire my dear.

CLAIRE and MARY curtsey. BYSSHE stands his ground at the back.

CLAIRE. My Lord —

BYRON. No request, no word! I am lathered, horribly.

Eyeing MARY.

CLAIRE. Mrs Mary Shelley. Mary, My Lord Byron.

Another curtsey from MARY.

MARY. My Lord.

BYRON. Mrs Shelley.

Takes her hand and kisses it.

I am cursed with a fool of a boating companion. The Lord keep us from the fantasies of our sycophants. There are some people who are like leeches, they hang on, you flick at them to brush them off, but they stick!

CLAIRE, looking round for BYSSHE, who hovers as far away as he can, glowering.

CLAIRE. And my Lord, this —

BYRON. Yes.

BYSSHE and BYRON stare at each other.

A younger poet.

A horrible silence. MARY and CLAIRE attempt to intervene.

CLAIRE. We —
MARY. Mr Shelley —

BYRON ignores them.

BYRON. What do you write on?

BYSSHE about to reply, but —

I write on gin and soda water. At night, 'til dawn. Damn important to pace yourself, I find. As the sun riseth so doth the gin in the glass.

A silence.

CLAIRE. Mr Shelley does not drink.

BYRON. Not another damn Wordsworth. I do distrust a sober poet who writes of nothing but ecstasy. Like a virgin writing hymns about the delights of a brothel. God's teeth! Bysshe

Shelley the wildman does not drink? What do we scribbling poets have in common?

Sir, you are silent.

A silence.

Sir, I do not know whether you are beginning to bore me, or to make me laugh.

A silence.

Sir, I have met this silence from fellow scribblers before. It usually means they think I am a bad poet. If that is why Miss Clairemont has affected this introduction then — I thank you for your spite. As a satirist, spite and hatred are meat and drink to me —

BYSSHE (*interrupting*). My Lord, you are a great poet.

MARY *and* CLAIRE *start and glance at each other.*

But you are an abominable sailor.

BYRON. Sir, what do you mean by that?

BYSSHE. I cannot see why you abandoned your barque in the hands of a fool.

BYRON. Ah. Ah. *That* — does call for an explanation.

Looking out.

That is my official biographer. Foisted upon me by John Murray, my publisher. Is Murray touching your stuff?

BYSSHE (*clipped*). No.

BYRON (*airily*). He will, he will. Commerce in the end hath every talent, raped up against a wall. Particularly when the talent is in the throes of divorce proceedings. A predicament that, I gather, is familiar to both of us?

BYSSHE. I do not hold with . . .

BYRON (*shouts out over the lake*). Polidori! Polidori!

(*To the company.*) The young shit hath a wonderfully ludicrous name, no?

(*Over the lake.*) Polidori!

(*To the company.*) He is also my personal physician. I am his sole patient. He has killed off all the others.

(*Across the lake.*) To the bottom, sir! Let the mermaids chew your bollocks off!

POLIDORI (*off, at the back*). I am trying hard, My Lord —

BYRON (*to* BYSSHE). Are there?

BYSSHE. My Lord?

BYRON. Are there mermaids in lakes?

BYSSHE. If a rhyme is needed, no doubt there can be.

BYRON. Indeed.

He laughs.

Indeed! I see I am talking to a fellow professional! So, you sail?

BYSSHE. Yes.

BYRON. Well?

BYSSHE. Yes.

BYRON. Excellent. You swim?

BYSSHE. Yes.

MARY starts.

BYRON. Well?

BYSSHE, *a shrug.*

Excellent.

They stare at each other.

You called me great. One is always pleased to receive a good review. For writers in our position, a good review is as rare as a double-yolked egg at breakfast.

BYSSHE (*bitterly*). For me, yes, but not for your Lordship —

BYRON (*the airy wave*). The praise of critics is bought, bought and sold. It is all to do with fashion. When you have some fashionable reputation with critics, cash it in. Foist an outrage on the bastards. It may, sir, come as a surprise to you that —

BYRON *looks down, thinking. Then continues.*

That the epithet 'great' is contrary to my nature.

MARY *scoffs. They all stare at her.* BYRON, *with a bow.*

Madam?

MARY. I am sure, my Lord, that no one of this company is foolish enough to confuse 'greatness' with 'arrogance'.

BYRON. Ah. I will think on that.

A sexual look at MARY *from* BYRON. CLAIRE, *trying to get over the hiccup.*

CLAIRE. But there is a touchstone. Shakespeare was 'great'.

BYRON, *up again.*

BYRON. I am loathe even to apply it to Shakespeare. A grotesquely talented little shit in the pay of royalty. (*To* MARY.) And yes, yes, I am in the pay of my publisher, Mr Commerce.

The look from BYRON *again,* MARY *dead still.* BYSSHE *sees nothing of this. He flares.*

BYSSHE. Shakespeare did not go far enough! Further than any of us can go, but not far enough! King Lear himself, not Gloucester, should have been blinded, and by his own hands. Then in his darkness he should have turned on God himself.

BYRON. But at least the bugger wrote a great deal! The greatest sin in a poet is anal retention.

BYSSHE. Explain —

BYRON. I have heard of this habit that certain madmen have from the pathetic Polidori. (*To* CLAIRE.) It would seem that some mad people are obsessed with their own shit.

CLAIRE, *mouth open,* MARY *takes a step forward but she says nothing.*

(*To* BYSSHE.) They tighten their arseholes day and night, to retain their turds. Which they do, for weeks.

BYSSHE, *enthusiastically.*

BYSSHE. I have heard of this too! What could release them from the infirmity, is the shock of electricity —

BYRON, *ignoring this.*

BYRON. Yes yes, but certain poets are turd retainers. When, after months, their bowels squeeze open, all they lay is a turd. Which they invite the public to see as a fertilized egg. With the purity of pure hatred, shall we name names?

BYSSHE. Why not?

BYRON. William Wordsworth!

Robert Southey!

We all, of course, write for love. But love can be a soggy dough. A little hatred is yeast and salt —

BYSSHE. You are wrong about Wordsworth.

BYRON. Yes yes, it is boring to be so wonderfully wrong about so wonderful a poet. I hate his guts. But — I give up. He has sold too many books. The poison of his works has, irredeemably, infected the bloodstream of our literature. You disagree. You know his poems, no doubt by heart.

BYSSHE. Those written before 1802 —

BYRON. Ah! Before reaction got him! Before he went religious. The rats! The rats! The rats that leave the revolution's ship! For the comfort of the Church, or some concocted mysticism, or good reviews in the *Times Literary Supplement*, or the Oxford Chair of Poetry! Sir!

He stares at BYSSHE.

You are serious. But a bit of a bitch too. There may be something in you. Dinner! Tonight!

Turning.

All of us, in my rooms.

CLAIRE. George —

BYSSHE, *over her.*

BYSSHE. Thank you, my Lord.

BYRON. Eat fish, d'you? Being vegetarian?

BYSSHE. No.

BYRON. Damn pity. Hired a man to catch trout in the lake for you. The lazy fella's at it now out there, if Polidori's not scared all the fish to death. No matter. (*To* MARY.) Maybe the women'll fancy a peck at it.

MARY curtsies.

MARY. My Lord.

BYRON. My dear Shelley you may have all the nuts and broccoli you can devour.

He pauses.

I have read you, sir.

BYRON *extends his hand. He and* BYSSHE *shake.* BYRON *holds on to* BYSSHE's *hand.*

I particularly admire your entry in the register of the hotel. 'Name: Percy Bysshe Shelley. Profession: Democrat, Philanthropist and Atheist. Home address: Hell'. I know you wrote it in Greek, but do you want to be eaten alive?

BYSSHE *wants to withdraw his hand, but* BYRON *still holds it. Then* BYRON *kisses* BYSSHE's *hand.* BYSSHE *recoils.* BYRON, *bowing to all in turn.*

My dears! Dinner! Dinner! Dinner! Tonight, tonight!

A gesture at the lake.

> If my biographer's body is washed up on this beach, drowned, send it back to England, suitably decomposed.

> *He has a hip flask in his hand. He strides away, drinking from it.* CLAIRE *runs after him.*

CLAIRE. George, my dear —

> BYRON, *viciously, into her face.*

BYRON. Dinner, dinner, at dinner!

> *They stare, faces close.* MARY *and* BYSSHE *have seen and heard the exchange.* BYRON, *airily to them.*

> Life goes on!

> *He goes off.* CLAIRE *at the back, looking at the ground.*

MARY. Drunk.

BYSSHE. Brilliant.

MARY. Brilliant.

BYSSHE. Drunk.

MARY. And silly.

BYSSHE. But himself.

MARY. And —

> *A nod at* CLAIRE.

> Brutally cruel.

BYSSHE. But we have met.

MARY. Yes! Now it has happened we can make it all mythical!

BYSSHE. Quite! We met naked —

MARY. At sunset —

BYSSHE. Maidens twined flowers about our hair —

MARY. Autographs were given to mermaids —

BYSSHE. Byron left on the back of a dolphin —

MARY. And Shelley?

BYSSHE. Ah! Shelley — erected an electrical machine and sucked the soul of Byron into a bottle! Screwed tight! Which he then did mix with a magic liquid, and drink, so Shelley too could have fame and money —

MARY. Embellish the scene!

   CLAIRE *turns, flushed.*

CLAIRE. Did you see how he did love me, wonderfully?

   A silence.

BYSSHE. Claire —

MARY. My dears, I think it best in matters of love, that —

   She pauses.

   That we have a good time? Introduce pleasure, and who can tell the taker from the taken?

CLAIRE. Mary, sometimes you are most matronly and sensible, at others you are a dirty-minded bitch —

BYSSHE. The school rhyme! We heard the children sing!

   They look at each other, then come together and embrace in a triangle, dancing round, chanting.

All. 'Oh Lord Byron loves his sister
His sister his sister
What a dirty mister, dirty dirty mister
Lord Byron loves his sister
And they both lie *down*!
Oh —'

   POLIDORI *steps up onto the stage, soaking wet. They stop in mid-song looking at him.*

POLIDORI. Ah! Mr Shelley. I — er — have read your *Queen Mab*. Some of it is very well done, some of it slapdash.

   A silence. Then SHELLEY *whispering inside their circle.*

BYSSHE. A critic! A critic!

CLAIRE. Ugh! Ugh!

BYSSHE. Ugh! Ugh!

CLAIRE. A slimy thing.

BYSSHE. Out the slimy sea.

CLAIRE.
and   } Ugh! Ugh! Ugh!
BYSSHE.

MARY (*through giggles*). Doctor Polidori, sir?

POLIDORI. Madam — I — who the pleasure — do I —

CLAIRE. We are Mr Shelley's concubines, sir.

BYSSHE. Run sir, these women have drunk the milk of paradise!
   No man's spunk is safe!

POLIDORI. Indeed —

MARY. Forgive us sir, our high spirits —

   She leaves the circle.

POLIDORI. At once madam, of course. Though it is not advisable
   to cavort so on a public beach.

   He looks around.

   There are tourists with spy-glasses. Er —

   He puts a hand out.

   William Polidori.

MARY. Miss Claire Clairemont.

   CLAIRE *curtsies.*

   Mr Shelley.

   BYSSHE *walks away.*

POLIDORI. I seem to have —

   He shakes his arm, it drips water.

CLAIRE. Lost Lord Byron?

POLIDORI (*turning in panic*). Oh my Lord!

   And BYRON *limps and stumbles back on. He ignores*
   POLIDORI.

BYRON (*to* BYSSHE). This damn hotel — we will move! I will

take the Villa Diodati. The poet Milton stayed there, perhaps the wallpaper is conducive to good verse. There is a smaller house, five minutes walk away. I suggest you, Miss Clairemont and Mrs Shelley take it, that Polidori here will do the business arrangements, a summer lease —

BYSSHE. I —

BYRON. No no no, we will summer together! It has hit me sir, an idea sir, we will all go communist. We are upper class renegades, we can afford it. More tonight! Plans, plans, of changing the world, of ripping human nature apart, love and summer, tonight! At dinner!

He turns to go.

POLIDORI. My Lord you abuse me.

BYRON. My abuse is a gift. It will enrich your diary.

He goes off.

POLIDORI. I share his Lordship's confidence, you see. I do share it. Anything you wish of him — ask me.

Going off.

My Lord —

And he's gone.

CLAIRE. Can we — afford a house?

MARY. No.

BYSSHE. No.

MARY. But we will! Life —

CLAIRE. Goes?

BYSSHE. On! On! On!

They move toward the circle again.

Scene Three

— *But* BYSSHE *walks away between the two women and goes off.*

Bright sunshine, green leaves. Pathways and vines between the Villa Diodati and the small house, Montalégre.

MARY. You were with him, last night, up at the big house?

CLAIRE. Oh yes!

MARY. Slept with him?

Nothing from CLAIRE.

We go back and forth upon these paths between his Lordship in Milton's old house and our — modest abode, every time of the day. But what do we say to each other?

CLAIRE. It is lovely this summer! It is lovely!

MARY. Have you told my Lord Byron?

Nothing from CLAIRE.

Have you told him you are to have his child?

Nothing from CLAIRE.

Claire, my dear, my darling, your mother married my father. That makes us sisters, yes. Also we are in love with the same man —

CLAIRE. Mary, now —

MARY. You deny you slept with Bysshe?

Nothing from CLAIRE.

You deny you still sleep with him?

CLAIRE. You — are with him every night!

MARY. But we all walk out, in the daytime, in the fields, along the shore, in an infinite combination of couples —

CLAIRE. Yes!

A silence.

We make love in the open air. Among the vines. On the stones. Or no, Bysshe and I do not make love, in the open air, among the vines, on the stones.

MARY. All I want to say is that, because of the higgledy-piggledy jumble, tumbled confusion of the state of our affections — I do not think I can bear — to have to be your mother too, my dear Claire.

They look at each other. Then laugh.

CLAIRE. Mary, Mary —

They embrace.

MARY. He —

CLAIRE. He? Which 'he'?

MARY. George Byron. He is the father of your child?

CLAIRE. Oh yes!

Realises.

Oh yes, Mary.

MARY. Tell him.

CLAIRE. I will.

MARY. Then claim the child.

CLAIRE. Oh no. George Byron will make me his wife. I will claim *him*.

A silence.

MARY. Claire, claim the child. For his or her sake, for your sake.

CLAIRE. But he will marry me!

MARY. How do you know that?

CLAIRE. Because of the manner in which I oblige him.

MARY. Claire, Claire —

CLAIRE. You will see tonight, at dinner, how his affection hath deepened.

MARY. How we do trust 'our affections'.

CLAIRE. What else can we do, all of us, in our predicament?

MARY (*to herself*). He hath no affections.

CLAIRE withdraws.

CLAIRE. Do not speak of George that way.

MARY. No I do not mean George Byron.

CLAIRE. Who then?

MARY. A figure.

CLAIRE. Mary, what is the matter?

MARY. Nothing it's silly, silly. I am writing the story of a monster. Very very silly!

CLAIRE. Monster?

MARY. He lives up in the snow, in the mountains.

CLAIRE. And he does not love us?

MARY. No.

CLAIRE. Maybe we will summon up your monster tonight, after dinner! Or Bysshe will, with electricity!

MARY. Or — he will come of his own accord.

CLAIRE. Mary! How beautiful you are, beautiful and strange.

They link arms, and —

Scene Four

Night. Lightning, thunder, rain.

Then, with candelabra standing about the stage, BYRON, BYSSHE, CLAIRE *and* MARY *lounge on the big cushions.*

BYRON *has a large brandy glass and decanter, which he dangles and pours from throughout the scene.* MARY *and* CLAIRE *drink wine.* BYSSHE *drinks water.* BYSSHE *is reading. He knows it by heart, and looks up after a few lines, to give himself time to think of what they say.*

BYSSHE.
There was a time when meadow, grove and stream
   The earth and every common sight
     To me did seem
   Apparelled in celestial light,
The glory and freshness of a dream.

A silence.

It is not now as it hath been of yore; —
   Turn wheresoe'er I may,
     By night or day,

A silence.

The things which I have seen I now can see no more.

Shades of the prison house begin to close
   Upon the growing Boy,
But he beholds the light, and whence it flows,
   He sees it in his joy —

A silence.

At length the man perceives it die away,

And fade into the common light of day.

BYSSHE *closes the book, pushes it from him. A silence.*

Whither is fled the visionary gleam?
Where is it now, the glory and the dream?

A silence.

BYRON. Yes yes yes, yes yes yes — *but!*

He pours a large brandy.

God's teeth Bysshe, must you after every dinner, dish me out these great slabs of Wordsworth? Like the slap of a cold fish in the face?

MARY. It is your medicine, my Lord.

BYRON. S'truth, I love they who love my health, but it is hard to take. Why? Why do you admire this dry-arsed poseur's lines so greatly? You are a publicly declared revolutionary. A communistical personality if ever I met one —

A wave of the glass at MARY *and* CLAIRE.

Willing to share your all, with all and sundry —

CLAIRE. } George —
MARY. } My Lord I do not like that —

BYRON. Brandy, brandy, brandy talking, no offence, *but!*

Charm. Smiles.

This is ridiculous. I sit here in the company of this rabid, militant personage, and he quotes England's most reactionary poet into my face. (*To* BYSSHE.) You admit the poem you quote is of defeat?

BYSSHE (*carefully*). Wordsworth does not think it is — but, yes, it is a poem of defeat.

BYRON. No no no, I'll pin you down. Are not the lines you just quoted aching with a middle-aged regret for the loss of youth's fire?

BYSSHE. Yes.

BYRON. You realise the poem argues that a five-year-old knows more than any twenty-five-year-old, let alone a thirty-five-year-old. Did Socrates talk rubbish from when he was six?

He groans.

I can even quote the bloody thing now from heart.

Trailing clouds of glory do we come
　　From God, who is our home:
Heaven lies about us in our infancy!

A silence.

Why do you not throw up? It is nonsense! I am agnostic, but you are an atheist. It denies experience, the maturity of manhood —

Another wave at MARY *and* CLAIRE.

And womanhood —

MARY *and* CLAIRE, *nod, at each other.*

CLAIRE. Thank you very much sir —

MARY. Very very much, sir —

BYRON (*with malice*). You do know about Willy Wordsworth, don't you, you know he was a Jacobin, that the light shone from Robespierre's arse for our William, when *he* was young? That he was in Paris, at the height of France's revolution, and thought the Terror a wonder of human excellence? *And* while there, got a girl pregnant, in the shadow of the guillotine? Met her once. Thin, long dank-looking black hair, horribly attractive actually, her name was Annette. And the child? Ah! Ah! Ah! If you want to utterly destroy William Wordsworth in conversation, ask 'Where are the children of the Revolution now?' — I did. His eyeballs burst with hate and guilt. What, what, what do you admire there?

MARY. Feeling.

BYSSHE. Yes. Song.

A silence.

BYRON. You defeat me.

MARY. The poem's argument is wrong, but its song is true. Truer than its argument. So why is there any difficulty — in singing it?

BYRON. Ah! Ah! Ah! Romanticism rears its ugly, look-both-ways, have-it-both-ways head! Though something be nonsense, feel the feeling.

MARY. But you have been called Europe's greatest Romantic poet.

BYRON. Slander! Slander!

He looks at his glass.

It may sell books, but slander! My favourite poet is Alexander Pope.

BYSSHE *about to explode.*

BYSSHE. Unreadable! Unspeakable, rhyming tinsel to flatter the ruling class, against life, I mean, I mean — the language deformed, prostituted, stuck in obscene corsets —

BYRON, *airily.*

BYRON. Read him every night myself. To clear the air. Yes, he was a deformed little dwarf of a man — but honest to himself. To what he knew.

BYSSHE. So is Wordsworth, in tonight's poem! Honest to himself! Are you?

A silence.

BYRON. Ah.

MARY. No, Bysshe.

BYSSHE. In what you write tonight, will you be honest to yourself?

A silence.

BYRON. I do not know, Bysshe. What I write tonight will, I am afraid, write itself. I will not know its worth, let alone its honesty.

A silence.

But if you write tonight, you will. My dear Bysshe, my dear, dear Bysshe Shelley. True poet.

He raises his glass.

But I do wish you were a fellow piss-artist. Drunkenness would give you a flair for publicity, if nothing else. And you would not drink water and quote Wordsworth late at night. Eh? Eh?

He looks around at them. They are all looking down.

God, you radical communards. I fumble a compliment to the poet among you, and I do not know if you be offended, indifferent, or moved. What matter, what matter.

CLAIRE. Moved. We are moved.

MARY, *looking up.*

MARY. But what matter?

BYRON *and* MARY *look at each other.*

BYRON. Perhaps, in the end, nothing. Or everything. I could end up believing not this, not that, but that *everything* is true. 'Everything is true' — what, pray, is that philosophy?

BYSSHE. Liberalism.

BYRON. Am I that ill?

MARY. You have symptoms, My Lord.

BYRON. A political pox, eh?

CLAIRE, *looking down.*

'Everything is true'. But for tyranny. Against that, I will take up the gun.

BYSSHE. I know you will.

BYRON. Mm. Mm. Mm, mm! I begin to enjoy myself greatly with you lunatics.

They all laugh.

Claire, my dear?

CLAIRE *crawls to* BYRON, *they put their arms around each other.*

'Crawling between Heaven and earth'. The shitty Shakespeare's line.

He pauses.

'Crawling between Heaven and earth.'

The line is meant to be a horror, but it is strangely comforting. I do not know why.

MARY. Because it sings.

BYRON. Ah.

A silence.

I do believe I have just lost a literary argument.

BYSSHE, MARY *and* CLAIRE *glance at each other.*

(*To* MARY.) Madam, last time such a thing happened to me, I fought a duel! Pistols, dawn, a secret field, all formality!

MARY. Name your weapons.

BYRON. Mm — rhyming couplets?

MARY. Refused.

BYRON. Your choice.

MARY. Wait

She thinks.

Home truths.

BYRON. I — am dead.

They laugh. Thunder, lightning. POLIDORI comes on. He stands, swaying over the lounging group.

POLIDORI (*aside*). I entered the drawing-room of the Villa Diodati. Outside, there raged the storm. No. Outside the storm raged. No. Outside, the storm abated. No. Outside, the storm I had just left, rolled around the gloomy house. No. No. I was wet and miserable.

He looks around the group. BYRON and CLAIRE kiss passionately. MARY shifts toward BYSSHE, turning the pages of the Wordsworth. They do not respond to POLIDORI's presence.

In a flash I saw them, a flash of lightning. The air in the room was heavy with their illicit sexuality, they had been at it, I knew it, I knew it, I knew it! They had thrown their clothes back on, the minute I came to the door! No. The two great poets, were, I observed, in contemplation, the women observing a discreet silence.

MARY turns, she and BYSSHE kiss passionately. POLIDORI flinches.

No. The profligate would-be poets and their, their whores, lounged upon the floor, and felt disgraced at my entrance, for I brought with me the wind and the rain.

He looks from couple to couple.

No. I am so lonely. Why do they assume I am second rate, when I am, not! When I am not second rate? I mean, has Shelley ever had a good review in his life? As for my life, I have never done one thing that is not decent, to anyone; or going on middling to decent! And look at them. Byron is an overweight alcoholic, Shelley is an anorexic, neurotic mess! The planet is bestrewn with their abandoned children, lovers of both sexes and wives! Shelley has tuberculosis, Byron has syphilis, and these are the men whom the intelligent among us worship as angels of freedom. No. It was a privilege to be the friend of those two young, beautiful men, in the heyday of that summer. No. Yes. After all, I am paid five hundred pounds, by Byron's publisher, to write a diary of this summer. Dreadful time, no! Time of my life. My decent life. So!

The couples finish their kisses.

I entered the living-room of the Villa Diodati, that stormy night.

BYRON. Polly, Polly, Polly Dolly dear, have a brandy.

POLIDORI. Lightning! Over the lake!

BYRON. What, sir, are you watery again?

POLIDORI. I was in it!

MARY. The lake or the lightning?

BYRON. I was about to say that —

MARY. But you did not.

   MARY and BYRON laugh.

POLIDORI. A storm like that, is like God. His hand, from the darkness, fingering his creation.

BYRON. Do not speak so in this company, Polly. With these free-thinkers, they who believe in God go straight to hell.

POLIDORI. I — think the image perfectly fine. The fork of lightning —

   He dangles his fingers to demonstrate.

Playing over the water and the mountains, like the Creator's hand.

BYRON. They who live by images shall die by them.

   Looks into his glass.

That *is* the brandy talking.

BYSSHE. Shall we go out?

   Stands excitedly.

On the lake, tonight?

MARY. Electrical experiments, Bysshe?

CLAIRE (*to* BYRON). Bysshe once flew a kite in an electrical storm, with a cat tied to it.

BYRON. A cat?

BYSSHE. The aim was to galvanise the animal's nervous system.

POLIDORI. I have seen this in madhouses, in France. There was much experiment in the French Revolution, with the mad. The jolt of electricity — to re-align the vital force, through the organs of the body.

BYRON. Ye Gods! You medical men and nature poets! Between you, will you torture us all to death?

CLAIRE. The idea of the cat —

BYRON. The cat aloft!

CLAIRE. Was that the animal be transformed, by natural force —

BYRON. And what was the result of this advanced experiment? Did the dog star bark at the poor pussy?

BYSSHE. The cat fell in the farmyard pond and drowned.

BYRON. A feline Icarus —

BYSSHE. Shall we go?

MARY. If you wish —

BYSSHE. The phosphorescence of waves may well be electrical, what if lightning link with it — and flash across the water —

MARY. Will you come with us, My Lord?

BYRON. I — think that on a vile night, such as this, I prefer the flash of brandy along the waves of thought in the brain.

MARY, *slyly*.

MARY. The unreal to the real thing?

BYRON. What do you seek to imply?

CLAIRE. The shadow to the substance?

BYRON. Are we talking about Plato's cave, or not gettting wet?

MARY. I, myself, have always been afraid of the story of Plato's cave.

BYRON. Why afraid?

MARY. There is something dark — something sinister about it.

BYRON. But Madam, two thousand years of philosophising rests upon the parable of Plato's cave. It is meant to be the great statement of the predicament of mankind.

BYSSHE. Let's do it!

BYRON. Do it?

BYSSHE. This drawing-room — make it the cave.

BYRON. Ah! Now! House party games —

   CLAIRE, *clapping*.

CLAIRE. Oh good, good, good, games!

BYSSHE. Where is Plato's *Republic*?

He scrabbles amongst the cushions. He finds The Republic. BYRON, *an imperious gesture*.

BYRON. Give it to me. I will read Socrates.

MARY. No sir, you will read Glaucon.

BYRON. But he says 'Yes Socrates' all the time —

CLAIRE. A secondary rôle will do you good, George.

POLIDORI. What — what is afoot —

MARY takes the book from BYSSHE.

BYRON. You are to be chained, Polidori, hand, head and leg, in the great cave of philosophical mystery.

POLIDORI. I — protest — I —

BYSSHE. The fire in the cave!

BYRON. Candelabra!

They move the candelabra to the front of the stage. N.B. the light from a footlight throws all their shadows onto the wall.

CLAIRE. Sh! Sh! The voice of the great philosopher, Socrates.

MARY reads: deep voiced, grave, strange.

MARY. In a dark cave sit prisoners. Their legs and necks are chained, so tight they cannot turn their heads.

BYRON. Polidori! At last a rôle in life!

POLIDORI. No, please!

BYRON whipping off a belt, approaching POLIDORI.

BYRON. You're going to love this, Polidori! Bysshe, a hand in this torturing!

BYRON *and* BYSSHE *manhandling* POLIDORI, *sitting him down, facing the back wall, tying his hands behind his back.*

BYSSHE. The human condition, doctor!

BYRON. Have him in rags, whipped and scourged or at least debagged!

POLIDORI. No no!

BYRON *into* POLIDORI's *ear.*

BYRON. Sir deliver yourself into the hands —

He indicates BYSSHE.

Of this advanced experimenter, about to fly you on some metaphysical kite sir, this very stormy night. Sir take the risk, your very being may be electrified into a cinder, you may fall from the sky into some muddy, farmyard pond — but you will be transformed!

POLIDORI. I will argue philosophy — but I do not wish to come to any harm.

BYSSHE *laughs.*

BYRON. What, you think philosophy, you think poetry harmless sir? Sir it can maim, it can mutilate, it can imprison men, women and children, blinded for centuries, it can kill. Sir, I thought you an intellectual — do you not know ideas can kill?

CLAIRE. Sh! Sh! The philosopher.

BYRON *and* BYSSHE *lay back, leaving* POLIDORI *upright, hands tied behind his back. His shadow looms on the wall. He tries to move his head, he cannot.*

MARY. Behind the prisoners, there is a fire. The light of the fire throws the shadows of the prisoners on the wall.

POLIDORI, *little jerks of his head.*

POLIDORI. What? What? What?

MARY. Between the fire and the chained prisoners runs a road. Along the road go men and animals. The prisoners see the shadows on the wall.

CLAIRE. Bysshe!

First CLAIRE *then* BYSSHE *cross the stage, distorting their arms and bodies into shapes that cast shadows on the wall.*

They combine to form animals — birds, cattle, a giraffe.

BYRON. Damme, what animal is that?

CLAIRE. A giraffe, obviously!

MARY. Now tell me, can the prisoners see anything of the men on the road, except for the shadows cast?

BYRON. No, Socrates!

MARY. And so they would believe that the shadows, and the shadows of themselves, were real?

BYRON. Yes, Socrates! Inevitably!

MARY. But now, what would happen to them if they were released from their chains and cured of their delusions?

BYRON. They would go mad, mad, mad!

CLAIRE. Keep to the text, George.

MARY. Suppose one of them were let loose, made to stand up, turn his head. And walk toward the fire. Suppose he was told that what he used to see was mere illusion, do you not think he would be at a loss?

BYRON. Mad! Mad!

A glance from CLAIRE.

Yes, Socrates.

MARY. And if he looked directly at the fire would he not be blinded?

BYRON. Yes, yes Socrates!

MARY. And if he were dragged up out of the cave, and saw the sun, would he not be in terror?

BYRON. Yes yes yes yes! Socrates!

MARY. And now I tell you, our real sun is but the fire in the cave. We are as distant as the prisoners, chained before shadows, as we are from the true sun. Which some call God. Which I call absolute good.

She closes the book.

BYRON. If I were such a prisoner, tell ye what I would do. Bribe a guard. For a gun. Blast my way up out onto the hillside. And make love with the first man, woman, boy, girl or animal in sight! Ye Gods! And *that* dismal parable, is to

date the greatest philosophical account of the condition of
mankind? The world is bloody — and real — and we know it.
Why torment ourselves with ghosts?

CLAIRE. But what would you bribe a guard with?

BYRON. My arse, madam, if need be!

CLAIRE. I see.

BYSSHE *flares up.*

BYSSHE. The fire in the cave is the past, by which we see now.
The sun on the hillside, is the future of mankind. It is our
future that is the absolute good! Plato himself was a prisoner,
religion a flicker in the cave! The mind of man, that is the true
sun! We are the instruments of that future light!

BYRON. You are spitting over us, Bysshe. I have noted the more
abstract you visionaries become, the more are we all drenched
in saliva —

POLIDORI, *suddenly.*

POLIDORI. I!

They look at him.

I — cannot turn my head.

BYRON. Don't be a fool, sir.

POLIDORI. I — am frightened what I shall see!

BYRON. Sir, turn your head. Leave visions to the like of
Mr Shelley here. Remain in the realm of the mundane, where
you belong.

*A pause, then POLIDORI turns his head without difficulty.
Crestfallen he shuffles away on his knees. BYSSHE's shadow
now dominates the wall. MARY looks at it.*

CLAIRE. There there, Polly —

POLIDORI *shrugs her off.*

POLIDORI (*to* BYRON). What — pray what, can you do better
than I, when it comes down to it! But for writing verses?

BYRON. Sir, first I can hit with a pistol the keyhole of that
door — secondly, I can swim for miles in the open sea — and
thirdly, I can give you a damn good thrashing.

POLIDORI. How dare — how dare — how dare —

CLAIRE releasing POLIDORI.

CLAIRE. There there, we are only playing, doctor.

MARY. At shadows.

BYSSHE (*to* MARY). What?

MARY. Your shadow.

BYSSHE turns, looks at the wall.

CLAIRE. Turn round now, doctor, you'll see a ghost!

POLIDORI jerks his head and looks at the shadow. BYSSHE moves into a monstrous shape.

MARY. What if —

She pauses.

What if a shadow that we made, upon the wall of our cave —

She pauses.

Stepped down? Walked toward us? Begged — for life?

She pauses.

And we gave it life. What would it be?

A clock begins to chime sedately.

BYRON. Ha! Ha! Midnight! Capital!

He slaps his thigh.

The sun is the other side of the earth, my dear Shelley. Your future's sun? Who knows whether it will give us dawn at all? Let us forget rational, electric experiments and go out — to open graves?

MARY, to herself.

MARY. The hideous phantasm of a man stretched out — but not a man, a thing, put together out of graves — by unhallowed arts —

CLAIRE (*to* MARY). Monsters? (*To* BYRON.) Monsters?

She giggles.

BYRON. Of monsters, this is the worst.
Coleridge's witch.

Beneath the lamp the lady bowed,
And slowly rolled her eyes around;

Then drawing in her breath aloud
Like one that shuddered, she unbound
The cincture from beneath her breast;
Her silken robe and inner vest
Dropt to her feet, and in full view,
Behold! her bosom and half her side —
Hideous, deformed, and pale of hue —
Oh shield her! Shield sweet Christabel!

He pauses.

Mm. Well, that is what opium doth for a poet. (*To* POLIDORI.)
In your role as a doctor, you do not have a quantity of that
wondrous substance about you, by any good fortune?

*Suddenly BYSSHE is seized by a fit. Mouth torn open — no
sound — he doubles up tightly and falls on his side.*

BYRON. Sir what philosophical point do you seek now to
demonstrate?

MARY. Don't touch him! Doctor —

CLAIRE. Oh Bysshe —

POLIDORI, *frozen.*

BYRON. Damnation sir, move to him!

POLIDORI. Yes yes, a rule, a rod, a stick, against him biting his
tongue —

CLAIRE *and* MARY *scramble about.*

BYRON. What in Heaven's name is the matter with him?

POLIDORI. A seizure My Lord, with this I *am* of some worth.

CLAIRE *hands* POLIDORI *a pencil.*

But an overloading of the nerves, an excess of agitation in the
fluid of the spinal chord — (*To* BYSSHE.) Sir, this between
your teeth, sir!

BYSSHE *stands suddenly and looks at them. A silence. Then a
thin, high sound from him, staring at MARY. He runs off, the
thin sound becoming a screech.*

BYRON, MARY *and* CLAIRE, *frozen.* POLIDORI *turn to
the audience.*

(*Aside.*) Followed him into another room. Calmed him. And
he did confide in me, yes, the 'great' Shelley, he did tell me of

what he had seen! He had looked at Mrs Shelley. And there, standing in her place, was another woman he had known. Naked. With eyes in her nipples, her nipples as eyes, staring at him! Is there no end to their fantasisms? To the indulgence of these revolutionary apostles, with their lives falling apart, their minds in rags? But I did write my account of the evening down and had it printed, in a book! It did bring me a little fame. I left them to their summer. To their diseased imaginations.

He goes off. BYRON, MARY *and* CLAIRE *stay, and* —

Scene Five

BYSSHE *alone. He laughs.*

BYSSHE. I am an atheist, who is haunted by the spirit world! How can this be?

Low.

The — worst ghost I have seen. The most horrid. The most — real — is a phantom that is exactly myself.

He laughs again.

We haunt ourselves. With man-made tyranny.

Even love is sold. Love withers under constraint. Love is the very essence of liberty — we constrain it by the feudal savagery called the institution of marriage. We haunt ourselves, with the ghosts of what we could be, if we were truly free!

Scene Six

BYRON, *coiling a rope.*

Sun and wind. MARY *and* CLAIRE *on a beach,* BYRON *and* BYSSHE, *later, in a sailing boat.*

CLAIRE. I found a letter Byron had written, to his sister, Augusta, it was obscene. It was magnificent.

BYRON *calling, off.*

BYRON. Bysshe! For godsake, are we going on the water? Or are you falling about in another visionary fit?

CLAIRE. The things he wrote to her —

Quoting, by heart.

'Naked — in your arms — no other love for me in the desolation of Europe, desolation of my life — dear Augusta, we have a true marriage, sealed in Heaven witnessed in Hell, forever —'

MARY. You read a copy?

CLAIRE. He had not sent it.

MARY. Ah.

She laughs.

CLAIRE. But it exists, it is in the world.

MARY. He is a writer of fiction, beware.

CLAIRE. Do you mean he really doesn't love her, but cares for me instead?

MARY. Claire, Claire, for the daughter of writers and the mistress of writers, you display great ignorance. Or misguided faith —

CLAIRE. I will overcome his affections. I will use the child. I will — mould him. He will write to me, as he wrote to his sister — 'I wish to have you by my side, to swim with you in the clear water of the lake, naked with you at dawn, when the world is new and young' — that will be me!

MARY. He is a libertine, in love with life — capital letters. They who are in love with life in that way, cause only pain to those around them.

BYRON throws the rope off, BYSSHE comes on and catches it.

BYRON. I do suppose I am the father — of Claire's coming little 'thing'.

BYSSHE. I do suppose so, George.

BYRON. I mean, to turn the conversation man to man — you have had 'em both, have you not? In your time?

BYSSHE. Rest assured that you are the father of Claire

Clairemont's child.

BYRON. No no, don't go huffy! It's all the same to me, m'dear fella.

He laughs.

Seems that you are intent on populating the world with ghosts, I'm intent on populating it with Byron's bastards. Damme! Why don't I stick to boys? Are we going to sail this bloody boat?

BYSSHE *pulls the rope.*

BYSSHE. Yes, there is hope for a storm!

BYRON *and* BYSSHE *work the rope, as they would a sailing boat, the rope taut between them.*

MARY. Augusta is his distant star. In whosoever's arms he lays, each night, he can look up and say 'There is my true love' — not this woman, man, boy, with dirty feet and night smells. If Augusta were to leave England and come to him, with all the terrible cost to her, the loss of reputation and scandal — he would at once betray her. Probably with you.

BYRON. All very well the carnal act, the act of love, with women, but with a boy you do think — Goddam it, this is the real thing! You ever gone that sweet route?

BYSSHE. Not my nature.

BYRON. What?

BYSSHE. My nature!

CLAIRE. I will tangle him. I will wrench him. Are we not always saying to each other, the world is yet to be made, we are changeable, we will invent a new society and a new human nature?

MARY. A new human nature? Out of George Byron? My darling Claire —

BYSSHE *and* BYRON *raising their voices now, against the sound of a storm.*

BYRON. Tell you the sweetest thing, love of a sister. We talk frankly? Your sister, very fine, ever had her? Come Sir — between the waves and us, our little lusts in a boat!

BYSSHE. We must follow our natures, what more can we do?

BYRON. Y'bloody hypocrite! Where is your legal wife? In England! The two women you are with, Mary y'call your wife, Claire y'friend — concubines, sir! Y'mistresses, sir! All your idealism, revolution in society, revolution in the personal life, all trumpery! The practice of it, sir, the practice doth make us dirty, doth make all naked and bleeding and real!

Angry.

Y'damn theorising! All you want to do is get your end away. And you make bloody sure you do!

The storm.

BYSSHE. I do not care what I do to myself!

I do not, George!

Let's peel open our brains, find the soul itself! Let's blast ourselves with electrical force — cut ourselves open, wreck ourselves, turn ourselves inside out! To find out what we are, what we can be!

That is what poets must do!

I declare I am a public enemy
Of kingly death, false beauty and decay —

BYRON. Bysshe sit down you maniac, there are waves breaking over our gunnel —

MARY. It's no good Claire. You know it. We will go back to England.

CLAIRE. No, we'll stay here, summer will never end, I won't let it — I'll reach out and — hold it, pull it back.

MARY. Summer is over, Byron's new poem is finished and copied — by us. He wants Bysshe to take it, sealed, back to England for its publication. I tell you! When Lord Byron finishes a new poem, summer is truly done for.

CLAIRE. What shall I do? Where shall I —

MARY. Live with us. We will find a small house, with a garden, be quiet, you will have your child.

CLAIRE. I will not have it called Augusta. I will not, will not!

Storm again.

BYRON. Here, you have your adventure, sir! We'll have to swim for it. Come!

He throws the rope at BYSSHE *who clutches it to his chest.*
BYRON, *ripping off his coat.*

The boat is lost. Dive in sir!

BYSSHE. No!

Silence from the storm music and effects. BYSSHE *sits dead
still clutching the rope.*

When will the world marry itself?
When will the true family be
All of human society?

I write poems. But most of the world cannot even read.

So what can I do?

Act as if I were free.

Write, as if I were free.

And at once — the storm.

BYRON. The boat is lost, dive in sir!

Swim!

BYSSHE. Cannot swim! Cannot swim!

BYRON. Ye gods, y'lied to me sir, venturing in a frail boat, in
bad weather?

BYSSHE. Cannot!

Sinking!

Down!

Through the lampless deep!

Of song!

BYRON. Damnation then I will have to stay and hang on with
ye! Ha! God's teeth, will you do anything, my dear Shelley,
to create an heroic episode?

The effects die down. BYRON *and* BYSSHE, *confronting*
MARY *and* CLAIRE *on the beach, the men dishevelled.*
BYSSHE *sullen,* BYRON *in great good humour.*

(*To* MARY.) Thought the boat was awash and done for. Your
husband clings on to it like a leech, announces he cannot
swim, madam! That he'll go down with it. Then damn well
sails it head on into the waves and saves us both.

A silence.

Maybe it was not as bad as that. But! Come my loves, my
dears, clean clothes, brandy, refreshments, talk — and then we
will retire — to colour up the incident in our diaries! All is
well. All is well. All is well.

*A silence, then they all relax and move toward each other in
a circle.*

Blackout.

ACT TWO

Scene One

HARRIET.

I married a poet. Fine poet, was he —
name o' Percy Bysshe Shel-ley!

She giggles then backs away, frightened.

Men in the trees.

She calls out.

Shillin'? Shillin'? Want me for a shillin'?

Low.

Men in the trees, midnight London, Hyde Park, banks of the
Serpentine. I am most refined, *most* refined, yer want me fer
a shillin'? Go down all fours on a grass? Or shall I recite
tastefully, verse he did write for me?

'Whose eyes have I gazed fondly on,
And loved mankind the more?
Harriet! On thine: — thou wert my purer mind;
Thou wert the inspiration of my song' —

Tinkly stuff, in't it dear, rather my arse fer a shillin', dear?
I was but sixteen when I married the poet, sir, where is he
now? 'E is on the continent, sir, on the Con-ti-nont! With
sweet Mary, Mare-ree! Who calls herself his wife, though she
not be, I be, legal-ly. Though she be, intellectually, my
superior.

A hummed scream.

Mmmmmmmmmmmmmmmmmmmmmm —

Now I live with a soldier name o' Smith, but he has gone to
India, and I call me Harriet Smith — that none may know I
was had by the poet Shel-ly —

Cruel-ly —

Mmmmmmmmmmmmmmmmmmmmmmmm —

Spitting the lines out.

Who telleth a tale of unending death?
Who lifteth the veil of what is to come?
Who painteth the shadows that are beneath
The wide-winding caves of the peopled tomb?
Or untieth the hopes of what shall be
With the fears and the love for which we see?

Pretty, pretty clever boy, Bysshe!
Ti-tum-ti-tum about death!

All that we know, or feel, or see,
Shall pass like an unreal mystery!

She blows a raspberry.

Yer want t'know 'bout death, mister poet, you go whorin' fer
a shillin' in midnight London!

Dialect change again, quoting her suicide note.

My dear Bysshe, let me conjure you by the remembrance of
our days of happiness — I could never refuse you and if you
had never left me I might have lived — but as it is I freely
forgive you and may you enjoy that happiness that you have
deprived me of — now comes the sad task of saying farewell —

She giggles.

Now I'll go for a swim, go for a swim, like a little girl, by the
sea-shore — wash off the men, swim, I . . .

She drowns.

Scene Two

Winter. MARY *and* BYSSHE *in winter clothes.* BYSSHE *carries
a book in his armpit and logs under his arm. He is reading a letter
that* MARY *has just given to him.*

BYSSHE. A month ago.

   A silence.

   How can that be?

   A silence.

   She drowned. And I was not told.

   A silence.

   Oh the circumstances — Hyde Park, that filthy, filthy lake —
   and, and —

MARY. Pregnant. (*To herself.*) Bad news. In England, on a
   dull afternoon, in a cold, wet garden.

   BYSSHE *flutters the letter.*

BYSSHE. I but wrote a casual enquiry to Hookham, oh, dear
Hookham — how, by the way, is Harriet my wife, and my two
children? And back comes the reply — oh, she drowned
herself, a month ago.

A laugh.

He says it was even reported in *The Times*!

Reads. 'Found drowned'.

Found drowned.

MARY. We must not —

BYSSHE. Not what?

They stare at each other.

Tell you what we must do — take out an order for *The Times*.
I should study the reactionary press more! Then I will learn of
the death of those I love!

MARY. We must be careful, because of this terrible news. Careful
of ourselves.

A silence.

BYSSHE. Do you also see, from the letter, I have received a good
review in *The Examiner*? True, written by Leigh Hunt, a
'good' friend of mine, therefore corrupt, but a good review!
What news! A good review and the death of my wife. Is
not life full, and wild, and a glory, and —

MARY. Stop it! You indulge yourself.

BYSSHE. Indeed?

They stare at each other.

Look, I was going to make a fire. For our little William and
Clara, in the woods, and roast chestnuts and tell them stories
from the flames, of spirits, and — make them laugh and
wonder —

He drops the wood at his feet.

It is Harriet's family behind this! The vile, the abhorred
Westbrooks! They did not tell me, so my silence would appear
horrible. Why? They want the children. The Devil! Why
cannot our children live with Harriet's? Why cannot I have two
families, or three, or four, what in nature forbids it? Ah,
English bourgeois morality, forbids it. What can a poet do,

confronted by the outraged, respectable English — with their bayonets of moral indignation fixed? I can hear Harriet's mother now, that thin, whining, hard done-by tone, all Christianity and naked malice. I am cast as a monster.

MARY. I too.

BYSSHE. It's all in rags, I —

A silence.

I have come to the opinion that there must be a revolution in England, I write for it, every morning, I —

A silence.

And my wife is dead —

He begins to laugh.

And my children stolen and —

Byron's mistress is about to have her child in my house —

House I live in with *my* mistress and *our* children — scandal, scandal, tittle-tattle —

And, in Ireland, English soldiers are murdering Irish liberty —

And, in my garden, neighbours peer over the fence hoping to see me, and Mary, and Claire, all naked, Claire with her big belly, rolling in the cabbage patch —

Quick, quick, inform the *Daily Mail*!

And in the foreign wars of liberation, as we agonise about who sleeps with whom, heroes scream under the torturers, and children pass their mothers and fathers the gun

Aie, aie! All is hysteria, is it not my love?

MARY. No. It is just The World.

BYSSHE. Just the world.

As I rhyme and rhyme each sunrise, of truth and the sublime —

As each midday comes, with farce, and mud, and the papers, and the post, all the opprobrium —

Opprobrium, good word, doth rhyme with bum —

Well, England! You neighbours, police committees, censors, you 'tut-tutters', you indignant dignitaries, parliamentaries, thin-lipped pedlars of smug moralities, I give you what you want, a shit-smeared bum —

Here, in rags, is the life we Libertarians lead —

Come! Wipe your arseholes! Be satisfied, justified, be *smug*!
I have my dead, but you have yours!

Mine, I will grieve for, s —

A stutter.

S — uffer the wrongs I did them, in p —

A stutter.

Private measure. But you! You great English, bourgeois
public! Your dead are at large. You pass them, everyday,
in the dirty streets of Manchester, of Birmingham, of London!
My ghosts will sing to me, but yours — will bury you!

(*To* MARY). Eh? No, my dear? Hey!

Shamefaced.

What sentiments, from — filthy, private things — to sedition
against my country?

Changes.

Do you think it took her long? It's not that deep, the
Serpentine, took the children boating on it once — S'only two,
three feet deep, the Serpentine —

Deep, in't? I —

MARY, *very angry.*

MARY. I will not have you, and I will not have myself,
condemned to this —

She pauses.

Raving in an English garden.

She scoffs.

The glory of the garden, in which the poet Shelley and the
women and children who love him are —

But weeds? Noisome, troublesome, scratchy, screechy things,
unacceptable —

BYSSHE. Unreviewable?

MARY. You have spoken, let me speak.

She pauses.

I will not have it. That we all be planted in the corner, as ugly — things, thistles, with poisoned spikes? Tolerated among the official flowers, all those pale decorated blooms of 'the nation'? I will not.

We have done nothing wrong.

Harriet was a fool to drown herself. Now that she is dead —

BYSSHE *stares at her.*

We can get married.

A silence.

Then, uproot ourselves? Plant ourselves abroad? Out of this —

A gesture, around them.

English garden, English graveyard? See, Bysshe! How to truly torture a metaphor, to its bitter end?

She pauses.

If we marry, the courts will give us your children.

BYSSHE. Harriet's children.

MARY. Children belong to no one, but themselves. As you have often said.

BYSSHE *wanders about, unable to reply. Then —*

BYSSHE. Neither of us believe in marriage!

MARY. You have married once already.

BYSSHE. But —

MARY. But?

BYSSHE. I have no defence.

MARY. You married Harriet Westbrook to give you and her what strength you could. You were both very young.

BYSSHE. Strength.

MARY. I want you to marry me. It is a practical matter. We must move through the world, armed as best we can be.

BYSSHE. You are very cold.

MARY. You are very callous.

BYSSHE. Why 'callous'?

MARY. Why 'cold'?

BYSSHE. My darling — well.

Laughs. Flutters the letter.

I receive news of the death of my wife, and you — propose to me? I mean —

He wipes his eyes, still laughing.

Are we really going to live this?

MARY. There lies your callousness, sir.

She curtseys.

For I live in your household. 'Sir.'

She curtseys again.

BYSSHE. Do not bob up and down like that, do not, I —

MARY. I — I — I — aye, aye, aye, yes 'sir' —

BYSSHE. Stop it! Now you! Stop!

Kicks the logs.

Light the fire, let the — little daemons dance, eh?

MARY. Retreating into poetic imagery again, 'darling'?

They shout.

BYSSHE. Will you marry me!

MARY. Yes! Will you marry me!

BYSSHE. Don't know!

They stomp around the stage angrily, avoiding each other and each other's glance. They calm down. BYSSHE *kicks the logs together in a pile. As he does so he smiles to himself —*

Mary, Mary, you are so fantastical, so — daring that I am ashamed, I —

MARY, *sarcastically.*

MARY. Quote:

My spirit like a burning barque doth swim
  Upon the liquid waves of thy sweet singing,
Blazing into the regions dim

Of rapture — with sails of fire winging
  Its way a-down your many-winding river,
I speed by dark forests o'er the waters swinging —

They glare at each other. A silence.

BYSSHE. Madam, you have been reading my notebook —

MARY. The bloody poem's about Claire! Isn't it!

BYSSHE. You —

He fidgets.

Have somewhat embellished it in the quotation —

MARY. Oh come on, come on! You wrote it, two weeks ago, after Claire sang us Mozart. And three nights ago you told me you wanted to sit up, 'To write'. Don't think you were a-writing, my dear, you were going a-down Claire's many a-winding river. In your boat. No?

Nothing from BYSSHE.

A heavily pregnant lady. But a woman, heavy with child, can with comfort and pleasure, have a man from behind. I should know. 'No'?

BYSSHE, *frozen.*

I do believe men call it 'spraying the baby's head'. Have you been spraying Lord Byron's baby's head?

BYSSHE. Yes.

MARY. Yes.

BYSSHE. Yes.

MARY. 'Course you have.

BYSSHE. Yes.

He pauses.

I —

MARY. The song you wrote Claire is very beautiful. As beautiful as her singing.

She pauses.

Will you marry me?

BYSSHE. Yes.

MARY, *without pause.*

MARY. Are you going to build the fire for William and Clara in the woods?

BYSSHE, *without pause.*

BYSSHE. I must! I've made up a story for the little man and little woman —

MARY. Light the fire, tell it to them, make up daemons, then come into the house — and have tea? Hot cakes?

BYSSHE. Yes!

MARY. Yes.

BYSSHE. Yes.

MARY. After all, somehow we are going to have to domesticate all these grand passions.

BYSSHE. Yes.

MARY. Yes.

They eye each other, beginning to smile.

BYSSHE. I'll go to London. Tonight, if I can book on the Post.

MARY. Yes.

BYSSHE. I'll file a suit for Harriet's children, in the Court of Chancery. Little Charles and Xanthe —

MARY. Yes —

BYSSHE. You and I will bring them up, with our children —

MARY. Yes —

BYSSHE. We will be one great family. And I'll see your father.

MARY. Ah!

BYSSHE. Ah!

They look at each other, laugh, then 'play act'.

I will ask your father, for your hand.

MARY. But my father, kind sir, is a rabid anarchist, much given against marriage.

BYSSHE. Not — !

MARY. Yes, kind sir, my maiden name is Godwin! Oh yes, kind sir, I am the progeny of that monster, he, to my shame, impregnated my mother —

BYSSHE. And art thou, then, horribly infected?

MARY, *a long curtsey.*

MARY. Oh yes, kind sir, see — my white limbs do shine with heresy, — my flesh is the false promise, to they who would be free — Can't keep this up! What's the best rhyme for 'womb'?

BYSSHE, *mock professional.*

BYSSHE. 'Bloom' as in 'flower'? 'Broom', as in 'brush'? 'Boom' as in 'bang'?

MARY. No, gerroff, sir.

In a deep curtsey, head bowed, her dress splayed around her.

Am I not thy tomb? Wherein thou wouldst lie, and gladly die?

She looks up laughing.

My father will be fine. If you give him a loan. Can you?

BYSSHE. I can — from Hookham. I'll exploit his guilt, at not publishing me. Thus, my dear, do we move the money of our friends around, to keep credit.

MARY. And flourish.

Standing, holding hands.

The fire, the children's story —

BYSSHE. Oh. I — yes.

He gathers the logs up clumsily.

MARY.?

They look at each other. BYSSHE *backs away. Stops. Then goes off, bent.*

The words.

A pause.

Oh, you can do the words, can't you, Bysshe. Quote —

Never will peace and human nature meet
Till, free and equal, man and woman greet
Domestic peace; and ere this power can make
In human hearts its calm and holy seat,
This slavery must be broken.

She snorts, very like BYSSHE *does.*

Now how about doing the life, kind —

The mock curtsey again.

Kind sir?

MARY *remains on stage. And —*

Scene Three

The crash of waves. BYSSHE *comes on with bags and rugs, which he piles before them.* POLIDORI *comes on, downstage. He wears a large black cloak which he wraps about himself. At the back, the* GHOST *of* HARRIET WESTBROOK.

POLIDORI. Dover Beach. Waiting for the packet boat to cross to Calais, and I see them! The Shelley menagerie, women, children, bags of seditious material, fleeing the country.

Now good Dame gossip doth say . . . That the Claire Clairemont woman gave birth to a child. Of my Lord Byron's. And the great Lord has taken the child off from the mother. Yes! And all were scandalised by the Mary Godwin woman marrying Shelley and trying to steal away the children of his first marriage. To bring them up atheist. But the Court upheld morality and said 'no'.

These people! Am I condemned to be the nobody at their feast? I will not make myself known. I will dog them. I'll send back tasty bits to the literary magazines. The Shelleys will belong to me.

BYSSHE. A stiff north-easterly! The captain is worried about sailing, there are ten foot waves in the Channel. I've told him 'We go, we go!' Come, bring the children.

CLAIRE. Let's have a ceremony! Scrape off the mud of our country, scrape off all the lies about us — yuck! All the muck of petty little minds. A grand farewell ceremony to England!

BYSSHE. I have already done such a ceremony.

CLAIRE. Oh? What?

BYSSHE. Written to my banker, telling him to pay no more bills.

Come! They are ready for us.

MARY *lifts a handful of sand and lets it run from her fingers.*

MARY. Disgrace. Exile. A holiday.

CLAIRE. Summer and hard light. And mountains in the sky again. Life will be a holiday, forever.

A change. A strangeness. BYSSHE *and the* GHOST.

HARRIET. Are you not taking me, Bysshe? I'll be no trouble.
I'll slip into the trunk with all the books, I'll be very small,
I'll sit on a spoke, on one of the wheels of the carriage, I will
hardly be there. Just — a patch, a little stain. Very faint,
very light —

BYSSHE. Yes!

A silence.

Yes. Why not?

He snorts.

Hasn't my life become a kind of haunting?

HARRIET. Has it? Oh, poor dear.

She giggles.

And —

Scene Four

1st May

Blazing light.

*From the travelling bags, they take white table cloths, books,
bottles of water, parasols. They take off their travelling coats —
light, summer clothes.* CLAIRE, MARY *and* BYSSHE *sprawl. It's
a picnic. The* GHOST *sits at the back, demurely.*

POLIDORI. And now they lie in the sun. In their rented villa, the
Casa Bertini, in the Appenine mountains. I mingle with the
tourists, look over the wall — whisper in the town 'They are
the creatures of Lord Byron, the rake, all of them — even
Shelley! He is translating Plato's filthy work, advocating the
love of men for boys.' Whisper — scandal — sweet, sweet.

MARY, BYSSHE *and* CLAIRE *with a mess of manuscripts.*
BYSSHE *correcting with a quill. They are in mid-flow.*

BYSSHE. You are both utterly, utterly, utterly, totally and
absurdly wrong!

CLAIRE. Oh.

MARY. Oh.

CLAIRE *and* MARY *laugh.*

It is always a very bad idea for lovers to start talking about what love is.

BYSSHE. All I am saying is, that we need a theory of the emotions.

CLAIRE. Why? Do we need a theory of breathing? If we did, with all the thinking on it, I believe we would choke —

MARY. Love is — 'The lineaments of gratified desire'.

BYSSHE. What?

CLAIRE. What?

MARY. A line by William Blake.

BYSSHE. That religious madman.

MARY. A *good* line. It means that 'love' can be anything. It shapes itself around the desire of the moment.

BYSSHE. Plato —

CLAIRE. Yes!

Claps her hands.

What does Plato say love is, Bysshe? You're just dying to get him in the argument!

BYSSHE, *rustling his manuscript.*

BYSSHE. The argument between Diotima and Socrates, which proves that 'Love is not a Divine God'. Shall we do it?

CLAIRE. Plato's *Symposium*, in the garden? What of the tourists?

BYSSHE. I will warn them.

Shouts, off.

Love is not a God!

The Greeks did it with boys!

POLIDORI *hisses.*

POLIDORI. Jealous, jealous, I am so —

MARY *and* BYSSHE *read — measured.*

MARY. Observe, then, that you do not consider Love to be a God. What, then, is Love a mortal?

BYSSHE. By no means.

MARY. But what then?

BYSSHE. He is neither mortal nor immortal, but something intermediate.

MARY. What is that, O Diotima?

BYSSHE. A great daemon, Socrates. He communicates between the divine and the human by science of sacred things, sacrifices, and expiations, and disenchantments, and prophecy, and magic. That is his daemonical nature —

He looks up.

Not a god, not a man, nor a woman, not a child, a daemon.

CLAIRE. Daemon —

BYSSHE. A force that flies between us.

CLAIRE. There!

MARY. There!

BYSSHE. There!

HARRIET. Pretty, pretty, how pretty, how pretty —

MARY *kisses* BYSSHE, *they lie in each other's arms.*

CLAIRE. I must go to Venice, Mary, Bysshe. We have not heard of Allegra, with Byron.

A silence.

I know he means to send for me.

MARY. I am worried about this constant travelling, little Clara is not strong, Bysshe.

CLAIRE. Then — my darlings, I must be with him. Why can't we all be together, as we were in Switzerland? That was a golden age.

MARY. Not really so golden, Claire, remember?

CLAIRE. But — we are all married to each other, is that not true? Plato's daemon —

She laughs.

Hasn't he run rings round all of us?

HARRIET. Pretty, so very pretty —

CLAIRE. I'll go. Alone.

A silence.

HARRIET. Pretty thoughts, of pretty people, pretty things. On the grass. Under the trees.

BYSSHE *suddenly stands.*

BYSSHE. I'll go with Claire.

MARY. Oh? Yes?

BYSSHE. We must bring George Byron to heel! He is behaving disgracefully. I'll go with Claire to Venice. I'll see him alone — and tell him what must be.

MARY. *You* will tell *BYRON*?

BYSSHE. We must be practical. What we want to live we must make — it.

MARY. I see!

She stands. Begins to pick up the bags and picnic things.

Well. Very well. You and Claire will go to Venice. And I will stay here and look after the children. Fine.

BYSSHE. We owe it to Claire. To Allegra.

MARY. Oh we do.

BYSSHE. Mary, please.

They look at each other. Then BYSSHE *puts his hand to her cheek.*

MARY. We were happy here.

BYSSHE. We will come back here. This will take but a few days, a week —

MARY. Fragile.

A silence.

I fear something could break. So easily. So — casually. Without us hardly noticing.

HARRIET's GHOST *hums a little tune, happily.* CLAIRE, MARY *and* BYSSHE, *still.*

POLIDORI. Yes! A little holiday in the Italian sun. Tracking down the literati, keeping track of their little affairs, their little sorrows. What greater delight? What better amusement?

Change.

I wish I was death, I would give them all a disease. They would hate me then, not ignore me. Not spin their 'new love' their 'new world' — they must not win. I could not stand it.

And —

Scene Five

August 23rd

Venice.

Rippling light.

BYSSHE *and* CLAIRE, *hand in hand.* HARRIET's GHOST *at the back.*

CLAIRE. The Grand Canal. My lover's palace.

She pauses.

Can a man love two women at once?

A silence.

BYSSHE. Can a woman love two men at once?

They look at each other, then kiss passionately. At the back HARRIET's GHOST *laughs. They part.*

BYSSHE. You understand why it is best. That I speak to Byron alone.

Pause.

CLAIRE. If Byron is — cruel about Allegra, will you make love to me tonight?

BYSSHE. Yes.

CLAIRE. Look at the light. It's going hazy.

She pauses.

We aren't on holiday anymore. I'll go back to the hotel.

BYSSHE. I'll come to the platform with you, for a gondola —

CLAIRE. Oh no. This is Venice. The city where young women go, stepping in and out of boats, between hotels — and palaces. You're so other-worldly sometimes, Bysshe — you haven't noticed the whole of Venice is a brothel.

She offers BYSSHE *her hand. He kisses it, fumbling. She sweeps away and off.*

HARRIET. Naughty naughty, naughty boy.

BYSSHE *turns round and pretends to throw something at the* GHOST.

Don't worry! When you touch her, tonight, you can remember touching me, and you will, won't you, husband.

HARRIET's GHOST *fades — and goes off.*
BYSSHE *alone on the stage, and —*

Scene Six

August 24th

The Palazzo Mocenigo.

Coloured light across the stage, as from stained glass windows.

BYSSHE *alone.*

BYSSHE (*to himself*). George Byron. I stand, a petitioner, in
   your marbled halls!

> *He laughs. Off,* BYRON *is heard rowing, there is a woman's*
> VOICE *and the sound of breaking glass.*

VOICE (*Italian*). Bastard! Bastard!

> *A crash.*

BYRON. Madam you are unreasonable!

VOICE. I will not have women in my household!

BYRON. Madam *you* are a woman and this is *my* household and
   you are, horribly, very much in it!

> *A crash.*

VOICE. Bastard English Milord! My husband he will *kill* you!
   Kill!

> BYRON *saunters onto the stage. He is in an elaborate dressing-*
> *gown. Carries a large bottle of red wine, is smoking a long,*
> *white clay pipe. His hair is dishevelled, his eyes dark with*
> *exhaustion. He is relaxed.*

BYRON. My dear Bysshe. Have my footmen not brought you a
   drink — carrot juice or something? The buggers are all drunk,
   no doubt. And it's only breakfast time.

BYSSHE. It is four o'clock in the afternoon, George.

BYRON. Yes yes yes. But I have finally gone day into night,
   night into day.

> *The woman's* VOICE, *off.*

VOICE. My life! My life! It is my life! I will *kill* myself, I will
   kill you, my husband he will kill us both, bastard!

> *A crash.* BYRON, *cheerfully.*

BYRON. God's teeth! Have y'had a married woman in Venice
   yet?

BYSSHE. We — I — only arrived this morning.

BYRON. Y'slow sir, slow! They marry young, to old noblemen, and there is a custom. I am the custom. I mean — they take lovers. It is an Italian institution. Her husband always knows, you go to dinner with both of 'em — You even ask his damn permission. The only right he reserves is to suddenly turn nasty and have you knifed and your body dumped in a canal — 'tis all exceedingly wearing on the nerves.

He looks at BYSSHE, *a silence between them.*

You damn revolutionist, carrot juice drinker. I am so glad to see you.

They embrace, BYRON *holding the pipe and the glass over* BYSSHE's *shoulders. They hold, then* BYSSHE *backs away.*

Forgive me, yes I stink of garlic. And my teeth are no better. *And* I had a particularly vicious clap last winter — nearly over that now, thank God. *And* my hair goes grey. Would dye it, but I keep on getting pissed and falling in damn canals! And how are you, my dear?

He eyes him.

In love?

BYSSHE. I — have translated Plato's *Symposium.*

BYRON. Not coming round to boys at last, are ye? Copy? Copy?

BYSSHE. Yes —

BYSSHE, *enthusiastically, takes a rolled manuscript from his shirt, and gives it to him.*

BYRON. A delight, a delight!

He puts it in his dressing-gown pocket and pats it. He pauses.

Nothing else for me? Out of the rotting north, the armed camp, the turgid cesspool — I mean England?

BYSSHE. No.

BYRON. I did think — perhaps you had letters — from Augusta.

Snaps out of it.

No matter! All that is dead. In a dead country. We are in the wide world now. Though —

Pointing the pipe at BYSSHE.

Beware, revolutionary. Venice too, is an armed camp. Austrian soldiers and spies everywhere. The city is not the cradle of civilisation, art and light we dream of. It rots. There is clandestine opposition, I do what I can, I flirt with it — is Italian liberty your cause?

BYSSHE. Liberty everywhere.

BYRON. Ha! Always the abstract. The real thing in Italy is câches of out-dated weapons, forever been turned over by the police, small meetings, infiltrated and betrayed, young men and women being beaten to shit in gaol. You want to get involved, I can introduce you to some people — poor Venice. A prison and a brothel.

BYSSHE. We noticed.

BYRON. Ah! 'We' again! C'mon, do not stand there so damn angelic, who are y'with, who are y'having?

BYSSHE. I came with Claire.

BYRON. Ah.

BYSSHE. She did your fair copy of *The Symposium*.

BYRON. Ah. The bitch was always good when one wanted something copied out. The damn bitch. She was . . .

A silence.

I shock you? Do not let this come between us, Bysshe, I will have none of it —

BYSSHE. I am a go-between.

BYRON. Nothing to go between.

BYSSHE. The child —

BYRON. My daughter, Allegra, is with me. And that is an end to it. I will have her sent to a convent. With a school. I have found the place.

A silence.

BYSSHE. Is that what you wish me to tell Claire?

BYRON. I wish you to tell my daughter's mother, —

An airey gesture.

Everything. Or nothing. What do I care?

BYSSHE. You are harsh.

BYRON. That is how it is.

He shrugs.

You reproach me?

BYSSHE. No.

BYRON. Damnation. Damnation. I know what you did for me, that she had the child in your house, that you give her a roof. But I have no endurance of these things, Bysshe, no endurance at all. It is not my behaviour that gives me pause, it is yours, my dear!

BYSSHE. Why mine?

BYRON. Ha! A little flicker of English puritanism there! You do reproach me, no matter. Your friendship is precious. Come, we will go out. I want to take you somewhere —

He pauses.

And show you something.

Scene Seven

November

Glittering light, haze. At the back, the huge shadowy image of a gondolier, slowly pulling at his pole, it looms towards us and passes.

BYSSHE *and* BYRON *lounge on cushions, as in a gondola.*

BYSSHE (*aside*). And so —

He pauses.

   O'er the lagoon
We glided; and from that funereal barque
I leaned, and saw the city, and could mark
How from their many isles, in the evening's gleam
Its temples and its palaces did seem
Like fabrics of enchantment — piled to Heaven —

BYRON *snorts, raising a glass.*

BYRON. Ha! You poor sod, y'believe in love, y'do, poor bastard. Yet you harm as many as I, you would-be 'moral immoralist'. You shred and tear lives around you as much as I, the cynic, the libertine. Yes, I leave my diseases in married bedrooms,

my children in convents — but you! What have you left?
A wife drowned in the Serpentine? And who was that other
little thing in London, overdosed herself with opium, because
of you? Oh yes, the appropriately named Fanny Godwin, your
second wife's little sister, all of fifteen wasn't she, when you
had her?

BYSSHE. I cannot be —

BYRON. Cannot be what? Responsible? Ha! My darling, darling
hypocrite. What a pity it is that you are not —

Wobbles his hand.

Turned the other way too, as I am. We could marry, become
two harmless old men, arm in arm on the sea-shore, writing
verse in peace, retired from this world — seething, organic
world, of flux, and blood, and manic husbands, and jealousy,
and babies bursting from wombs and aching cocks, eh?

He laughs.

D'you know where I found myself, one night last week?
Halfway up a drainpipe to the balcony of an eighteen-year-old
heiress. Dangling in mid-air, d'you know what happened
to me?

BYSSHE. The drainpipe gave way?

BYRON. Worse!

BYSSHE. Chest pains?

BYRON. Worse! I looked down into the street and there, dressed
for the opera, was the Venetian correspondent for the London
Daily Mail. Spotted! And then, ah then —

A silence.

BYSSHE. Well, what? Did you go up to love the heiress, or down,
to thrash the journalist?

BYRON. For a moment both delights had an equal attraction.
No. I despaired.

BYSSHE. Come, come —

BYRON. No no — despair. Perhaps it takes a high-blown, high-
flown personality, such as I have engineered, to be caught in a
scene of outright farce, to feel —

An airey wave.

That profound emotion. Up a drainpipe?

BYSSHE. A good story —

BYRON. Is it not, is it not. Actually, I went down and bribed the spy to silence. Now is *that* within my received character, yes or no?

BYSSHE. No.

He pauses.

No —

BYRON, *angrily.*

BYRON. Then believe what I say, you tight-arsed, 'Libertarian', 'free-lover', 'free-liver'!

BYRON *looks away, dangling his free hand in the water. A silence.*

BYSSHE. What are you telling me? You went home, reformed?

BYRON, *good humour back at once.*

BYRON. Not at all — waited 'til the spy was well away — then went to the servants' door — another bribe — and up to her. Sweet thing. Fair hair. Down on her thighs, unshaved skin — soft, like feathers. I am not telling you that I have reformed, I am telling you that I have despaired.

BYSSHE. What right do you have to do that? You do not have the right. Despair? Easy, George! Cheap merchandise for a writer. You will end up silent or making a pretty lyric out of the phrase 'I have nothing to say'.

The people of England — they may well have the right to despair. So would you — if you were a mill-hand in Manchester, or a child down a mine, or a mother to a labourer's children in a filthy hovel —

BYRON. Perish the thought —

BYSSHE. But for a poet to despair? Obscene! We claim to be the poets of the people of England. How dare we — luxuriate in denouncing the human cause as lost?

The great instrument of moral good is the imagination. We must not let it become diseased! We must be optimists for human nature!

    We might be all
We dream of, happy, high, majestical.
Where is the love, beauty and truth we seek
But in our mind?

Poets are the unacknowledged legislators of mankind!

BYRON. You talk Utopia. We are where I want to take you. Come on dreamer —

He stands.

BYSSHE. What is this island?

BYRON. A madhouse Bysshe!

He laughs.

Come on! We are the wide world's tourists, no?

The stage darkens.

Come on, I want you to meet a true 'citizen of the world'.

BYSSHE (*aside*). The oozy stairs.

Into an old courtyard. Black bars.
A face, looking down. Hair of weeds.

The intendent took us into that terrible place.

The madman sat by a window. He said —
'I met pale pain, my shadow'.

A silence. Then BYRON, *in the shadows, with the madman's voice.*

BYRON.
I met pale pain, my shadow.
How vain
Are words.
Oh — from my pen the words flow as I write
Dazzling my eyes with scalding tears . . .
What I write
Burns the brain
And eats into it.

BYRON *again as the madman,* BYSSHE *flinching away, as if approached.*

Sir, sir, kind sir — you have a childish face — sir, sir, a rhyme — of the fate of poets . . .

Most wretched creatures, they
Are cradled into poetry by wrong
They learn in suffering what they teach in song.

BYRON (*in his own voice. He laughs*). See, my dear? A poet in an asylum. Is he not a lesson to us all? A sweet irony, no, Bysshe? You write to change the world. And the world has its revenge — it overwhelms you with its cruelty.

The madman laughs, BYRON *laughs.*

Scene Eight

Light. BYRON *gone.* HARRIET's GHOST *at the back.*

Hotel room, CLAIRE *and* BYSSHE, *kissing. She backs away.*

CLAIRE. So Byron will not see me. So no matter!

   She spins, false good spirits.

BYSSHE. Why did he take me there? A joke? A warning? A —

CLAIRE. What of Allegra?

   Nothing from BYSSHE.

   What haven't you told me?

BYSSHE. Byron is putting Allegra in a convent, with a school.

CLAIRE. Oh no.

BYSSHE. He can, he's her father —

CLAIRE. Oh no.

BYSSHE. He has the right.

CLAIRE. Oh no.

   A silence.

   I'll — go to him. I'll dance naked for him, I'll paint myself,
   I'll let him put me in chains, any filthy thing he wants — I'll —

   She freezes, fists clenched.

   Not! No, I will not be — diminished by this. By the cruelty of
   a Lord. From now, I will look to myself.

BYSSHE. Yes.

   A pause.

   We — will conquer our fears.

   The GHOST *giggles. The light shifts. And —*

BYSSHE. I will have nothing of madmen. Poetic indulgence. I
will see the real world.

Scene Nine

November 1817

BYSSHE, *aside.* HARRIET's GHOST *at the back.*

BYSSHE. I can see it. St Peter's Field — the outskirts of
Manchester. A great crowd, some 60,000 working men and
women. Armed only with banners.

And then, from nowhere — the militia. The brutal attack. In
ten minutes, a massacre. Eleven dead, four hundred and
twenty-one cases of serious injury, one hundred and sixty-two,
men women and children with sabre wounds.

And where was I, the poet? Impotent in Italy, in the sun.

He turns. Hotel room. MARY *and* CLAIRE. *They are
awkward in their movements, distressed.*

The world is catching fire, the oppressors have bloodied their
hands! But what excites the educated classes? The behaviour
of the rich and famous in bed.

CLAIRE. Bysshe, it would be better if you did not talk. Not now.

BYSSHE. Why?

He looks at CLAIRE, *then* MARY.

What's the matter?

MARY. Ha!

A silence.

BYSSHE. What? Is little Clara worse?

It's nothing, a stomach upset, a cold on her chest. She's a
child of the new age, the dear little ones, they will have to be
tough as steel, soldiers, for what is coming —

CLAIRE. Be quiet, be quiet, can't you tell what has happened?
Are you so insensitive, isn't it screaming off us? Your daughter
died, an hour ago, while you were out in the street.

A silence.

BYSSHE. No, a little cold, and we are in Venice! A city of the
rich! Of hypochondriacs! Of art! And science! And light!
There are legions of doctors in this rotting hell, I'll go out,
get medicine, for a little child with a bad tummy —

MARY. Let me hit him in the face, let me pull out his hair,
scratch out his eyes —

CLAIRE. No Mary, stop it, stop it, stop it!

She restrains MARY, *who subsides.*

BYSSHE. I'll go and see her — kiss her, breathe life back —

MARY, *low.*

MARY. You will stay where you are. You will keep away, you will be still.

Utterly still.

A silence.

It was you who made me bring her to Venice. The cruellest thing you have done to me. Impossible, impossible journey, with a sick child —

BYSSHE. There was nothing impossible about it! I drew up a time-table! For the family, the servants, you had only to keep to it, it was all absolutely clear! There was no reason for anything to go wrong!

MARY. You accuse me? Do you come into this hotel room, dreary, dreary hotel room, find your daughter dead and accuse me —

BYSSHE. Yes!

You dessicated, withered bitch — yes!

He looks down.

I —

Low.

No, of course I do not accuse you.

MARY. I am glad to hear it, for I do accuse *you.*

CLAIRE. It's the grief, only the grief, the grief talking, please my loves, do not —

MARY. Accuse you. For the cruelty, pointless cruelty of all your schemes. The endless, mad-cap journeys, in the heat, in dirty coaches.

The endless —

hopeless —

schemes, and dreams, and —

She calms herself, then continues.

What have you achieved, Bysshe?

BYSSHE. I have written — of the Peterloo massacre. I have written 'The Mask Of Anarchy'. Let it be — a poem — for our daughter.

MARY. Oh! Can't you hear yourself? Do you know what you're saying?

Is the price of a poem — the death of our child?

'The Mask Of Anarchy'! No one will publish it. Will Hunt, in *The Examiner*? No, he knows he will go to gaol for seditious libel.

She scoffs.

The great revolutionary, English poem — unpublishable! Bury it in your daughter's coffin, poet.

BYSSHE. We do what we can! I write what I can, I —

He covers his eyes with his hands.

At the massacre — they carried the word 'love' on a banner.

MARY, *looking away.*

MARY. Oh yes, put the word 'love' on a banner, put the word 'life' on a banner.

CLAIRE. But we are still in love. We all are, with each other. The sorrow of this — will bind us together.

A silence.

MARY. Yes.

All still.

Yes.

CLAIRE *steps forward, hoping they will form a circle, as in earlier scenes — they do not.*

Scene Ten

July 1818

Beach. The Gulf of Spezia. Crash of waves. The stage empty.
BYRON *and* BYSSHE *walk on.*

BYRON. A newspaper.

BYSSHE. Yes.

BYRON. Run — and written by us?

BYSSHE. A voice in England — radical, fierce, uncompromising —

BYRON. With wonderful reviews of our own work, no doubt —

BYSSHE. It will be a banner! A beacon! That is why I have asked Leigh Hunt to come out and join us.

BYRON. The worthy, boring, Leigh Hunt. I see you are as — hot as ever, my dear.

His eyes wander over the landscape.

BYRON. Our two boats moored up together! D'you think 'The Bolivar' is ostentatious?

BYSSHE. Highly, George.

BYRON. Good! You admire the brass cannons?

BYSSHE. Do they work?

BYRON. Work? What does that matter?

He laughs.

Do you like the moulding on the prow? Does it not make the boat look more fearsome?

BYSSHE. It is all excellent, George.

BYRON. As for your boat —

He sniffs.

Is she not shallow in the water?

BYSSHE. How could a boat named the 'Don Juan' be shallow?

BYRON. Cutting, cutting sir — was damn flattered you named her after my poem. I do not object to plagiarism — when it flatters.

BYSSHE. I am thinking of renaming her 'The Ariel'.

BYRON. Yes, more airy-fairy, more like you.

He looks away.

Your women, walking the beach, I see. Still the same menagerie. How is she?

BYSSHE. Claire?

BYRON. You know whom I mean.

BYSSHE. Changed. Well. Different.

BYRON. Much —

He pauses.

BYSSHE. What?

BYRON. After —

BYSSHE. Come, George! They have both had children by us, who died in this country, it is not like you to flinch from raising the subject.

BYRON. Allegra. That damn convent, I felt like breaking in, shooting nuns left, right and centre! Ha! And your wife?

BYSSHE. You know she miscarried a child? Two months ago?

BYRON. Ye Gods. Two men together, two women together, on a beach. But, but, but!

Slaps his thigh.

We have not met enough, Bysshe. What have we done for three years? Barged about this bloody country, you with your holy family, I with my whores. A prison of open air, hard light. I'm thinking of going to Mexico — there is a revolutionary war there. Or Greece. Though the Greek clap be just about the worst in the world — as I well remember. But all this writing about tyranny, eh? In the end you get itchy fingers. Violent verses pale. You want to actually put a bullet in a fat neck.

MARY *and* CLAIRE *walk on. They stop when they see* BYRON. CLAIRE *goes to turn away,* MARY *stops her.*

(*To* MARY.) Madam. (*To* CLAIRE.) Madam.

MARY. My Lord.

She curtsies. CLAIRE *does not.*

BYRON. Well! Shall we all dance upon the beach again, my loves? Shall we send up Shelleyan balloons, loaded with lightning experiments? Steal some fire? Shall we, eh?

MARY. Forgive me. I am not too well, today, My Lord.

The two women walk by them, and go off.

BYRON. A war. If only there were a war in England, not that endless — slow, sullen defeat. Why don't the bastards take up arms against such a government? Then we poets would be of some use, we'd do the songs, the banners, the shouts, but no. Sullen silence.

He pauses.

Is Williams down there re-rigging your boat?

BYSSHE. I want it to sail faster.

BYRON. Huh!

BYSSHE. I will race 'The Bolivar' to Livorno, when we go to pick up the Hunts.

BYRON. Oh the Hunts, those bloody children, why do these well-meaning literati have so many of 'em? All so healthy, and so — eh? I am so damn restless.

They look at each other.

Well, well! Let's go play with our boats, like good little boys.

He stomps off. BYSSHE *stays on the beach. Then* MARY *and* CLAIRE *come on.*

CLAIRE. Do you know, that is the first time I've seen him — since our daughter died? Is that not terrible — or farcical? He looks crabbed. Much older.

MARY. What of the plans with the Hunts?

BYSSHE. We will sail both vessels to Livorno. You stay here. We will bring the Hunts — if things can be made quiet, between them and George —

MARY. Why cannot they come over land?

BYSSHE. We — will sail. Jane Williams would very much like to sail, perhaps —

MARY, *bitterly.*

MARY. Yes. Jane Williams.

BYSSHE. What is the matter?

MARY. What can be the matter?

A silence.

BYSSHE. Williams is re-rigging for me. I must go and help.

A silence.

We are well! It will be fun!

He goes off.

CLAIRE. Jane Williams, his boatman's wife?

She laughs.

MARY. Have you not listened to the pretty little love lyrics, being read each night, after supper, as if out of thin air?

She laughs.

And — I found the manuscript of the new, long poem he is writing. At the bottom of the page, in tiny, tiny writing, were the words — 'Alas, I kiss you Jane'.

CLAIRE *looks away.*

CLAIRE. Not to be diminished. I will join —

She pauses.

The subterranean. The subterranean community of women. I'll travel. I'll see Islands. And the snows of Russia. I will never marry, for I was married once.

She looks at MARY.

To you and to him.

MARY. Do you know what the new poem is called?

CLAIRE. No.

MARY. Guess.

CLAIRE. How can I?

MARY. Guess! Guess! Guess!

CLAIRE. Mary, stop it —

MARY. It is called 'The Triumph Of Life'.

She doubles up, shaking with laughter. CLAIRE *does not laugh.*

'The Triumph Of Life'! 'The Triumph Of Life'! 'The Triumph Of Life'! 'The Triumph Of —'

And —

Scene Eleven

The stage darkens.

POLIDORI *walks about the auditorium, a glass of wine in his hand, wearing a smoking jacket.*

POLIDORI. Oh yes, I knew Shelley in Venice well, oh yes, many an evening, went to brothels together, talking literature the while, oh yes, Shelley's mistress, had her myself, oh yes yes, 'course I was the model for the diabolical, in Mary's novel, oh yes, had her, many-a-time, gave her the plot for the damn book — yes, no, well not quite, but to all intents and purposes, I saw Bysshe Shelley jump into his boat, in Livorno Harbour, with the storm coming, my opinion? Suicide, yes, no doubt, an utterly unstable little prick, y'get m'innuendo — yes, I'll have more wine, kind of ye —

Wandering out of the auditorium.

Yes, m'literary reminiscences, course y'know about the body when it washed up? The fish had had the eyes out, and eaten the testicles, what dinner? Kind of ye, most —

He has gone. And —

Scene Twelve

BYSSHE. *A sail. Dark stage, his face. NB. No 'storm effects'.*

BYSSHE.
As I lay asleep in Italy
There came a voice from over the Sea
And with great power it forth led me
To walk in the visions of poetry

I met murder on the way —
He had a mask like Castlereagh —
Very smooth he looked, yet grim;
Seven blood hounds followed him:

All were fat; and well they might
Be in admirable plight,
For one by one, and two by two
He tossed them human hearts to chew
Which from his wide cloak he drew

And with pomp to meet him came
Clothed in arms like blood and flame
The hired murderers, who did sing
Did sing! Did sing! Did sing!

He pauses.

And Anarchy, the ghastly birth
Lay dead earth upon the earth,
The Horse of Death tameless as wind
Fled, and with his hoofs did grind
To dust the murderers thronged behind

A rushing light of clouds and splendour,
A sense awakening yet tender
Was heard and felt — and at its close
Words of joy and fear arose

Men of England, heirs of Glory,
Heroes of unwritten story,
Nurslings of one mighty Mother
Hopes of her, and one another;

Rise like Lions after slumber
In unvanquishable number —
Shake your chains to earth like dew
Which in sleep had fallen on you —
Ye are many — they are few.

He pauses. A change.

The waters are flashing,
The white hail is dashing,
The lightnings are glancing
The hoarspray is dancing —

The Earth is like Ocean
Wreck-strewn and in motion:
Bird, beast, man and worm
Have crept out of the storm —

A silence. A change.

When the lamp is shattered
The light in the dust lies dead —
When the cloud is scattered
The rainbow's glory is shed —

Change, at once.

And 'fear'st thou?' and 'Fear'st thou?'
And 'Seest thou?' and Hear'st thou?'
And 'Drive we not free
Over the terrible sea,
I and thou?'

He pauses, and to a broken, odd rhythm.

Mother of many acts and hours — free
The serpent —

These are the spells —
    by which to reassume
An empire o'er the disentangled doom.
To suffer —

    woes which hope thinks infinite
To forgive wrongs darker than death or night
To defy power which seems omnipotent —

To love, and bear —

    to hope till Hope creates
From its own wreck the thing it contemplates

This is —
    to be
Good, great, and joyous, beautiful and free.

Sh! Sh! 'voluptuous flight'   'volup — tu — ous flight!'

He laughs.

Ha! An easy rhyme there — with 'night'.

A blackout.

And —

Scene Thirteen

A blast of storm effects — briefly — they die down, the lights come up. At the back, HARRIET's GHOST. BYSSHE's body is furled in the sail upon the stage. BYRON stands behind it, looking at it. He keeps his distance. The GHOST stands at the back.

BYRON. We'll burn the body on the beach.

    I loved him.

    Thus is another man gone, about whom the world was brutally mistaken.

    And in the name of all the mercies, look what the sea did to his flesh.

He shouts.

Burn him! Burn him! Burn him!
Burn us all! A great big, bloody, beautiful fire!

A blackout.